# Cheap Therapy

Naveed A. Khan

ISBN-13: 978-1-477-44868-7
ISBN-10: 1-477-44868-3

For Nanu.

You are missed.

# Sections

Acknowledgments    i

Counting Raindrops    7

Shadows of Imaginary    61
  Friends

Cheap Therapy    125

The Rage of Achilles    185

# Acknowledgements / Preface

First, I'd really like to thank my laptop for not dying on me midway, with all the dozens of open tabs and applications I've had running all at once. Next, I need to thank all the local Tim Horton's shops in my vicinity. Mostly because I'm not making star bucks yet to be drinking coffee regularly from Starbucks. I'm also particularly grateful to all the heartbreaks for providing me with such great reserves of inspiration.

I would like to thank a lot of people, too. First, my parents for their care and support. Thank you for understanding my decisions. I would like to thank the few friends I keep very close to me for their continued presence around me, though I understand how much of a pain it may be at times. But thank you for putting up with me – you know who you are. A huge thank you to Ehsan Rajeeb Sarder for the cover photography. You don't know this, but you've left a lasting imprint on me since my childhood, so thank you for allowing me to idolize you for a good half of my life. Lastly, a heartfelt thank you to Kaitlin Elliott for being such an amazing friend and my human diary. You have been the major driving force behind me completing this project and have been more excited about it than I have. Thank you, thank you, and thank you – all of you.

*

Some say I'm crazy, others might say that I'm overly ambitious. I find the two to be synonymous. Even then, both these traits have proven to be more of a strength than a weakness. I wanted to have something with my name on it before I turn twenty-one, so this is my first attempt in breaking out into the literary world.

One of my favourite poets, Shihan, is National Slam Poet Champion and has been featured in Russell Simmons' Def

Poetry Jam. In one of his Def Poetry performances, he managed to define what a poet really is. He said that "poets write poetry because they can't afford therapy." With that, I found a heightened purpose in writing. However, over time, writing became more than just a therapeutic outlet. It became a lifestyle for me. And I sure as hell couldn't afford therapy, but I could always afford to write.

I don't believe in censorship because I've been taught the value of honesty. With that being said, you may or may not like what I've written or even like me for that fact. But I've learned to write for myself. And I've also once  heard someone quote that "to be a writer is standing up to get shot at."

These are beyond my own stories, they are also stories of other people, who I prefer to leave anonymous out of respect. They are my documentations of life in the only way I know how: through words. They are fragmented glimpses of thoughts, emotions, people, places and events. Any similarities to individuals living or deceased are not merely by coincidence.

Indulge in my words at your own discretion.

*Cheap Therapy*

*This is probably haram.*

*Naveed Khan*

# Counting Raindrops

## Vulnerability

Vulnerability is, for some reason, often looked down upon. As if some unforgivable crime has been committed, and put on trial and sentenced to scorn and judgment. Why? How far of a deviation from your socially accepted norms is it to actually be able to feel and express abstract thoughts and emotions? I would say that to allow one's self to be vulnerable takes more nerves than when being peer pressured into substances. These are my words. I wrote them for myself and have chosen to make them available for others to read if so they wish. Judgment doesn't affect me.

## Material

The mind, it wanders towards doors of which the doormats do not bear the words of welcome. It would be fortunate if there were mats at all. It is among these unwanted companies that one can truly learn the degree of reform needed in order to function accordingly and desirably with this class. This superficial status gained from material things. Those things stitched and stamped with, supposedly, any ordinary name, and sold at prices that make your organs groan in displeasure. It is no doubt a luxury that is fitting for those that work hard enough to earn it, however at the same time as easily accessible as candy to some others. However its not about the things, but rather the people. Because no matter how ironic the literal fact may be, that people make these things - in the end it is these very things that make people. It is the material impressions and the artificial personas that get people places in life. That's the sad truth. And for those that couldn't buy their way into the good pages of life, there's education, which ceases to work as well but serves as a fair substitute. So what am I doing all this for? In the end if it turns out I need more than just good credentials, a reference letter, and a degree, then what? Because I refuse to buy myself a living doesn't mean I'll accept the sufferance of neglected potential. No, I'm determined to define my own success.

## Unnecessary

Easier said than done. And more often are thoughts thought of without thoroughly thinking through them. On the contrary, at times there are particular thoughts that are better off not worth thinking about. These are the annoying ideas and the pessimistic scenarios that an overly over-imaginative mind may tend to draw up. Usually there's a certain trigger setting these thoughts off, but there are also those bizarre moments when they appear out of thin air.

These are the unnecessary thoughts. And as much as people may think otherwise, they are indeed unwanted. They are a sort of parasite that feed off the mind's greatest fears, and they multiply, and they linger. The objective of this virus is to continue its reign until you seem, to yourself, as mad, then soon followed by the public. This and many of its gruesome affiliated parasites, however, can be rid of easily. As the root of every problem is your mind.

Through analysis it can be concluded that in this case, the conflict in particular is none other than assumption. To make an assumption is to dive into murky depths of shark-inhabited waters and convincing yourself you'll leave unharmed. As a middle school band teacher once said, "To assume is to die. Never assume, know it."

## Desire

The heart wants more, but the mouth is too afraid to voice its desires. Afraid to hear it out loud and in the open air. Scared of what demons the utterance may attract. Careful not to shake the stars out of place or tempt the clouds to crash to the ground. Why, can these desires be so ill in will, or is it that they are perhaps too strong for any instrument to contain? Or perhaps the dangers do not as so much lie in the desires themselves, but rather in those desiring them. For greed, in itself, is a force of nature so vile it brings out demons in the holiest of saints.

## Being

I'm showered in raindrops as I observe the composition of my destruction. I can only wish that you would plagiarize my feelings and use them as your own; maybe then we would have enough in common to be happy again. But the fool in me placed happiness on a pedestal and this is his ultimate consequence. The lonely path that I am on is broken, and the fragments of brick and debris have cast dust into my eyes, and I am blind. I realize now that the world looks the same without you, but much, much emptier.

## Again

When there's nobody else around to pretend to, and the anger dies down, you realize that nothing has changed. You wish it did, but it didn't, and you're in the same place and position you left yourself in. You need more time. But time is slipping away from between your fingers. You need to catch your breath. Try opening the window, but you realize it's barred from the outside. You get up off your seat to walk to the door, but realize that your feet are chained and you fall face first onto the hardwood. You can feel yourself bleeding, you can feel the tears. When you open your eyes and pick yourself up again you see that the blood and tears on the floor have taken shape as the picture of her face, with nearly perfect detail. You want to scream. This is when you realize, you're losing your mind.

## The Broken Fry
*For the Ks*


The broken fry lay limp, disheartened and alone, drowning in sprinkles of his own salt and covered in a dash of ketchup. His temperature had fallen, and he knew it would be only moments until he would turn crispy and stale. Completely unwanted. He wished to call out to the stray leaf of lettuce lying a few inches away, but could not find his voice. It seemed they had lost the battle. It was over. The caloric crime scene of cholesterol consumption. $5.82.

## Visibility Restricted

Visibility restricted. That's what the sign on the side of the road said. It was a very official looking sign, printed in yellow with black text. So with both hands grasping the wheel, I closed my eyes so not to break the law. I have faith, I told myself. That is when almost suddenly, my world began to change shape. It felt as though my soul slipped out from between my breath and the wheels of the car. My hands had turned to ice and the vehicle began to drive itself. The dotted lines became hungry sharks swimming through the pavement, sending violent ripples of concrete in all directions. The street lights had become search lights with vicious lasers attached, scorching anything in its course. The road signs became swinging traps, teetering from one side to another with serious agility. Beyond these obstacles stood a man with a single hand outstretched. The car came to a stop just barely touching his hand. He wore a white beard, a red top hat and worn out overalls with seemingly nothing underneath. He said, "You're going the wrong way."

That's when I opened my eyes.

## Becoming Undone
*For Adiba H.*

Everyone's looking for love and attention
Maybe I should be different,
and look for hate and rejection

A box full of contempt, wrapped in paper with a bow
Swallow a couple hands full of regret,
like pills lined up in a row

Shoot my arm with cold nostalgia of days passed
And then come up to the surface
for a breath at last

An ice cube to go with this emptiness
To bring the chill and then
it's all gone again

And then I sit back and repeat all the steps through one
Take another shot of my thoughts
and become undone

## Social Insurance

Hypocrisy is the common denominator, "good" is a decimal place holder, and people are all numbers. Digits in a statistics report, monetary values, and net profit in a capitalistic world. Where your only identification is a government issued social insurance number, a.k.a. your dog collar, ID tag. They're not concerned with your name or origin or if the H is pronounced silent. The means by which you put food on the table, raise your family and send your kids to school. No. What they are concerned with is that you pay your dues in taxes, despite the fact that you might be struggling already. No! It's all for you, better roads and health care provisions! You can really see where your money is going when the roads aren't clean at ten in the morning after a whole night of snowing. Or in the way a woman, which could have most likely been my mother, loses her child while in labour and waiting in the emergency room for twelve hours. Wait. My taxes didn't pay for an extra bed and nurse? Or some fucking towels? Make budget cutbacks and yet more tax hikes. Call it something brand new and quasi-pleasant – like the Harmonized Sales Tax. Then while you're in office take your family to a beach resort in Cancun while mine struggles to pay property taxes.

What does my social insurance number do again? Is there even a plan I can choose for that shit? Can I at least pick my favourite number?

## Brave Heart the Businessman
*For Jay G.*

There is no plus side to minuses. A bank account polluted with overdraft transactions. The bills are piling up, and I've lost count of all my interest rates. I have a confession to make: I am a terrible spender. You could say, I wear my cheque book on my sleeves; always investing in markets that I can't even afford. But I've never penny-pinched a day in my life so I play my stakes for the highest stocks. Win or lose, drown or survive. My debt collectors know me well enough to bring a bottle or two every time they visit, and they sit inside and listen to the stories of my latest ventures. They call me fearless.

They also call me foolish.

## Defeat

The feeling of defeat is often familiar like a reoccurring nightmare. Its metallic, almost copper-like taste is a lingering one. It is one that does not want to fade. Like the smell of your hands after serving a withering woman paying $62.80 in change. You can taste the rust on her ancient coins with your fingers as you count and place each into their respective compartments in the drawer. You can taste it just like you can taste your own despair. The old woman is nobody to you, but she is the world. Despite the pains she has caused, you conjure a smile and politely hand her the receipt. "Come again," you say, apparently cheerful. And she will, and just like times before, soil your hands, and she will do it again. It is an odour that withstands even the most persistent use of soap. No, defeat does not leave easily. It will gradually subside.

But it will make sure you remember.

## Rest in peace(?)

Question: Do the deceased really rest in peace? Or do they still yearn for those they wished to meet, one last time. For proper goodbyes and a peace of mind. How does then one find peace when both parties are left in grief? Coffins or white sheets, ashes on the pyre or left to bleed like a soldier on foreign streets. They say don't cry so they can rest but maybe restless is what they want to be. Enough so to stir up a pulse and full body functionality. Reach out a hand and say, "I'm not finished, I've got more life in me." People will stare astonished as they say, "I just shut my eyes for a minute, I'll choose when I can leave." And the story of mistaken-to-be-dead people will spread across the seas. Newspaper headlines will read, "Because they couldn't really rest in peace."

## Liquid Spaces

It feels like I'm headed down a straight path to a crooked world. Where the oceans flood the sky and the stars are on the ground. A place with textures beyond the capacity of the sense of touch, filled with colours that aren't even real. Liquid spaces. Flowing with a mass fluid emotions that I never knew even existed prior to now. I'm afraid if I reach for something here, it will all shatter and I will have woken from a dream. But I know I am not dreaming.

I hate that the definition for ambiguity is in itself ambiguous. So, don't ask me how I feel. If I knew how I felt, I would be at least half way there to being alright.

## Vertigo

It feels like I'm about to board the last plane headed to nowhere. A one way flight to no way back. With the promise to break promises, a vow to never keep one. I close my eyes long enough to feel as if they're open, and open them to find darkness as if they were closed. A mind full of questions so simple they might as well contain the answers, but answers so complex that they are better off seen as questions. She found me lost in a place I thought I found. Displaced in this thing called time, white flashes contrasted with black dots. Images of a place so non-existent, that it once felt real. Happiness.

I am falling.

## Slippery Sleep State

Bathe in the blackness of your room lit by fatigue. Cringe in the wakefulness of an overactive mind; overly exerted but too stubborn to surrender to slumber. Sleep sprays itself upon your eyes intermittently, the greater force of it lapping against the shores of consciousness. Letting the cool substance drown your body, you feel like you're drifting further away from land. Floating. Your vision spins itself into something less real, yet still lucid enough to feel. Just as the currents cast you away, the tide washes you back to the sands of sleeplessness, where the nostalgic wails of shells cast a haunting echo that reverberates through you.

Sometimes, all you want to do is sleep.

## The Over Coat

As the sun begins to settle itself in the sky, I prepare myself for another day. Slipping on my overcoat, I observe the several missing buttons. I think about you and conclude, "If I slowly lose all my buttons you'll have none left to push." I stand before my mirror in a coat that can barely hold its ends together. This is a coat to keep me cold, not warm. And today, I'll lose another button.

# The Ocean is on Fire

The ocean is on fire.
Emotions burning.
Waves of hope
fried to a crisp,
and tides of joy
overdone until stiff.

The ocean is on fire.
Lit from gasoline
spills of guilt
and the sparks
from bright dreams,
that were left to wilt

The ocean is on fire.
Open for display
an all ages event
serving to portray
how feelings so fluid
can turn to cement.

When the ocean is on fire,
where will you find water
to put it out?

## Understand

I understand that it's hard to understand. That to understand is so subjective that it's fluid, yet expected to be solid like concrete. Comprehension is deceptive in that it is subjective to perception. All things seen or heard are not all things understood. All things understood are not always seen or heard. I don't understand. Nobody really does.

## No Littering

The sign said no littering so I decided to be a rebel and drop some subliminal garbage. Like the way they drop bombs overseas inducing the blood and the carnage. And if they point fingers to accuse me I'll say I didn't start it. That I was provoked by intentions that were long before tarnished. It's retarded, to discard my cognitive processes as trains of thought, when they are more like spacecrafts. Because the sky is not my limit; how the hell can you even say that? Because trains fall off track and my destinations are far. I'm trying to reach beyond the stars and come back with scars. And contusions, that bear signs of struggle and confusion and the way I've used them to push forward through your arrogance and nuisance. I keep my marbles in a bag; I'm too smart to lose them. And I'm not so great at art so I'll let you draw the conclusions. Words are lethal weapons, through misinterpretations and ways that we use them. Loaded with emotions, yet we continue to abuse them. They can build up, tear down, help heal and hurt. Deceit works subliminally through subtleties, like the subtle T's in words... I bet you didn't catch that, okay scratch that. I'll give you something else to lash at, like the fact that: I woke up one morning and realized I was straight. And I began to fear that gay people would be afraid and my friends would never treat me the same way. So I question the beliefs I once believed to believe in. I call my god an atheist because he doesn't believe in the ones that conceived him. I find myself bleeding, above all reasons, fiending for diseases they don't have cures for, like Jesus. Screw this no littering bullshit I don't need this.

## Weight of Words

The weight of words weighs heavy on hollow hearts and empty chests. Worse yet are the once that are loaded, destroying upon impact. Words like, *love* and *hate* and *want*. *Want* is such a greedy word. And *murder* sounds bloody murderous to me sometimes. And sometimes the word *sometimes* needs to happen more often. Like sometimes she'll say things that weigh more than a ton. But she doesn't. Maybe because those kinds of words are too heavy to lift off her tongue or bring forth from her brain or too heavy yet still to even think of them. Maybe she needs some help? Or maybe words don't mean enough or anything at all and she's smart enough to know this. Or maybe words are the greatest cures, to help heal people. Words like, *beautiful* and *amazing*. Or maybe at the same time the greatest weapons? Words like *hate* and *kill*. And threats like, "*weapons of mass destruction.*" They never did find them right?

Words.

## Portrait
*For Nyomie N.*

She has a quiet smile. The type that doesn't say much but says a lot. Her eyes are dark and mysterious, finely outlined so from different angles they resemble either ancient Egyptian or sometimes East Asian. She's the type to look away when she realizes her eyes are being watched; the windows to her soul are off limits. She sometimes wants longer eye lashes. Sometimes. Her skin is vanilla with just the slightest hint of caramel, and seemingly glows when angered to the right degree. Her hair is dark, with loud red highlights in the bottom layers. It looks better when she doesn't have it tied up. She's the strong and silent type. No, she's pretty talkative actually. But only when she wants to be. She's a book with no synopsis. She covers it with a smile, but I can distinguish her battle scars. Her smile is one smiled not from the eyes; just a calm surface masking an ocean of stormy secrets. She's happy. She's also a bad liar. She's doing fine. She will.

## Empty Sex

I used to be the kind of man to always have a plan. Until the day I ran out of plans, or my plans just ran out. Or, maybe I just ran away. You see, I had it down to the tee, from the A to the Z and it's hard to believe. But I did, and I'd like to say I still do, but I don't and it feels like I never will. But still, I remember someone once told me to think before I speak, and someone else told me I take too much time to think. I think, the best is to find an in between but I'm always stuck in between things I should never be between. People. I'm running on impulse, taken and swallowed all insults until my insides have indulged in pain to the point where they've become fully accustomed to feeling it. I have finally developed the immunity I need. And as such I have fallen out of love with falling in love. Whether it be a person or an idea, or an idea of being in love with a person. You could say I'm more in love with the prospects of hate and infatuated with lust. I have an admiration for beauty and a particular resentment towards trust. I am a weapon of war fully loaded with witty remarks and sexual humour, with my sniper scopes aimed squarely at women's behinds and bosoms and want nothing more than for them to feel as empty as I do. In our bodily exchanges we whisper things, only to later play them off as a product of only that moment, not knowing they are our souls' sole desires. But for the sake of our egos, they go neglected.

This is what empty feels like.

## Addiction

Call this addiction a failure of resistance. A lack of negligence for affection, which means you have my full attention. And if you were a glass you'd be full of it, spilling off the brim. And I'm just trying to get in like the pores under your skin. My mind is dim, but your shine blinds my optics. You're picture perfect, Kodak moment, no need to photoshop or crop it. The gradients of your radiance emit a hue close to that of gold, which implies you're hard to hold. Harder yet to let go.

## Psycho
*For A.S.*


You're psychopathic, sober-drunken-madness like the joker laughing. So vivid, manic, it's praise to call it graphic, ego crashing. Too much disgust to discuss or mention, not worth my attention. Perhaps it's pride retention, blowing off and relieving tension. People hated I never subjugated, instead I waited and learned a lesson, so fuck this mess I was never obligated.

## Human

Humans have been humanized through human eyes to realize human lies. Humans cry as humans die, and some human tears never dry. The pain resides locked up inside, infecting minds. Power, greed, and pride, and revenge as motives for crime. Believed to be at the prime, living on borrowed times. Every day more loss of human lives, children die, men abuse their wives. Struggling to survive, feed a family, keep lights on at night. Sometimes the glass is half empty, the tunnel too dark to see a light, and eyes closed tight even when it's bright. Woes and broken bones, children grown in broken homes, sometimes all alone left to take care of their siblings on their own. They seldom complain because it's what they're used to, and pursuits of school are most unusual. Yet we complain about what we have whereas they'd be blessed to, be in our shoes but they'll never get to.

The nature of being human.

## Phantom

This phantom is a menace. These nightmares are like tenants, in my head. Standing by me like a war lieutenant, I'm the commander-in-chief. I'm the bystander in grief, watching feelings retreat, and I let it. Waist deep waters, I am treading, dreading it but I meant it if I said it. So I hereby take full credit. These demons are crying to me, in reverie, rotting inside me like liver disease, and so are the memories.

## Absent Minded

I'm absent minded, sipping and relaxing on that gin and absinthe. It takes careful practice to get through my mind's elaborate labyrinth. Tactics to tackle the sickness I have witnessed and fell victim to, I need some prophylactics to prevent any further madness. I'm crazy enough to shake babies, call me Michael Jackson. This impractical sadness factors for only a fraction of what I lack, as I have admitted to. Administered the pain I need in order to gain a new level of sinister. Insane as a maniac, which I am in fact, I will not deny it. My mind is absent, I've given up trying to find it.

## A Little Truth

Some people constantly feel they need to act as if they have something to prove to the world. Not as something they can prove, but something they absolutely need to. These are often the pretentious few, with their condescending snares and that act as if they have their pinky up even while fucking. Truth is, they're the kind that lacks personality the most. They are this way, seemingly unknowingly; however they're at least somewhat aware of their falsities. That is when materialism takes over, the over-indulging in things valued at a lot but really worth nothing. Money, cars, clothes, social status, and even their seemingly witty remarks. A cover-up in order to drive the common eye away from the real gaps in their personalities, and ultimately their lives.

Don't you pity them?

## Turtles
*For M.S.*

I could tell, I told her, that she was the type of person to hang her dreams on a clothesline. So they can get some sunlight and dry away last night's tears. I told her she doesn't need to cry and she said she knows, pointing out the perfect example of the fact that we all do things regardless if we know better. We smiled and we took a moonlit drive past midnight, grabbing fistfuls of air until our fingers turned cold. She liked turtles. She told me they grow according to their surroundings but are happiest when able to live free without being enclosed and restricted. Kind of like us.

## Diagnosis

She kisses my forehead so gently it sends a shiver through my entire being. I was mistaken to have ever thought such a phenomena was impossible. It is then that I feel like my clothes have been stripped from me in broad daylight and it is her warmth that I currently bask in. When I open my eyes and look into hers, I see myself looking back as confused as I feel. Her eyes are like two small daggers waiting to tear a hole in my surface and uncover my secrets, but she is unsuccessful in her attempt and in return frowns. She says, "Take your time," and I very much intend to. She says I move her, but I hope not too much -- or she might be too far for me to reach. Her lips are like ambrosia, a drink of the gods quenching the thirst of my soul. She has opted for permanent residence in a place in the back of my mind and no eviction notice will remove her otherwise. "You're amazing." She smiles at me, and then I remember the reasons why I loved in the first place.

## Regret

Crawling under my skin, feasting on my soul. In the dark of the night, when no one else is home. The whole city's asleep and nobody hears my screams, and I've seen this scene so many times in my dreams. And now lone behold I'm living it, lord forgive me for having given in. You told me to count my blessings but I've been counting dividends. I live in sin, and ever since I lost my mind I haven't really been living since. I'm six feet under in a life full of blunders. Fool hearted and I love blindly like Stevie Wonder. I count rain drops when it thunders outside, and stay and watch as I leave my thoughts out to dry. No one on the line but I hear voices in my mind all the time. So much static and I can't drown out the noises. This regret is flowing through my veins like slow poison.

## STD
### (Secrets That Destroy)

You ever have those thoughts that you're too afraid to say out loud, just because you know how true they are? Knowing that in your head they're safer because once they hit open air it will take effect to ruining everything in your life. Those certain things that you know are so true in fact that it seems to you as if preventing their utterance will delay what you already know to be ultimately inevitable.

In reality, these are the kinds of thoughts that aren't safe even in your head.

## God

She found god in a credit card. The same one she used to buy her shoes. Designer purses, so worth it, not to get it confused. Figure fitting dresses, that her body just caresses. Let things determine her value, drinks screaming out expensive. Little does she know what she really has. She once found happiness but couldn't make it last.

She found god in a bottle. The same ones she downed every night. Said she needed a little something to make it feel right. Room spinning out of control, she jerks her head back. On the floor, down on all fours, she pukes it all right back. Regret down her cheek in the form of a tear. She grits her teeth, starts to scream and pull on her hair.

She found god in him. But that was the story way back. Used to kick it now and then, back when life was laid back. She was an artist and he made rap, always filled in what they lacked. She once let the four letter word slip, he said, "How the fuck can you say that?" She waited for the next words, they never came. Instead he backed up against the wall, the look on his face said he was afraid. She apologized and left and never showed her face. Premature confession, she wishes she could go back and erase. She couldn't make up her mind to whether or not to forgive him. See, she once used to love god, but she lost her faith in religion.

## Sleeping with Clocks

Every tick of the second hand strikes like thunder. The sound bounces off the walls and reverberates through my spine, sending a chill throughout my body. There are five clocks in the room. One mounted on the wall, one sitting on the dresser, two on opposite ends the desk and one on the shelf above the bed. That's five times the thunder, five times the chills. There's another on my bedside, but it's digital but it might as well tick its fucking life away too. My phone rests in front of it with an animated manual clock. This one ticks but makes no sound. It's taunting me.

I am awake, I am lifeless. I am constricted by time, unable to sleep.

Each clock is set to a different time, either ahead or behind. One only bears the exact time but I can't remember which. Two bear the same time but are placed the farthest apart, so that if I do catch sleep I'll have to endure the laborious task of shutting them both off.

The other clocks are set in a method to enable three to five minutes of snooze time between different clock alarms.

This is how a partial insomniac sleeps in order to ensure his ability to wake, lest he find sleep.

Clocks are whores. They'll sleep with anyone.

## Transparency of Wax Wings
*For Faria I.*

I'll swallow a fistful of the sun for you, and burn up all my insides. Wrap me in a cocoon of bandages, hold me in your light. See through me like you've known me all your life. This metamorphosis will take time, but I'll come out with new wings; ones good enough until I fly too close to the sun again. Swallow another fistful, only to be nurtured back to health. And I swear I'll do it all over again just to feel the look of your velvet eyes.

## Meredith

She's got a leopard print heart, god in her credit card. Dresses to look smart, talks it to play the part. Likes living large, online shopping cart filled with designer purses and satin scarves. She even pretends to really like art. She doesn't. The drugs take her to Mars, believes they can heal scars. But nothing will ever really relieve such a broken heart. Body shaped like an hour glass, but she never lets an hour pass. Too lifted to ever want to crash. Too drunk to even try to stand. She'll never understand. She's open to every friendly man with a bit of cash. Spends the night unable to rewind it back. But swears she'll do it again to feel anything but sad. Too much for her to grasp, but whatever she can of life she grabs. She kind of likes the candle light romance of pain, feels no shame in submitting to the other kind of fame. You can see it painted on her face; she's committed to the chase. Get up in the morning she'll be catching the first train so she has a little something to her name.

## Courage

I mean, we weren't all built like Adonises. But the compliments do help our confidence. Competing for competence while dismissing all consequence. Logic fails to conjure it, so the heart and mind are seldom congruent. Words sprinkled on like condiments. Same words semi-reversed to play condolence. For our old selves, rested on old shelves. Changed well far beyond what time can tell. Lost moments for forced ones, for stunning endorsements. We're all whores, son, running solely on endorphins. The metamorphosis below the surfaces, turns all life into carcasses. Hollow hearts harvesting feelings for the catharsis. Mark it, for the markets. Determine the key targets. Mass produce, but you've got nothing to gain if you have everything to lose. But sometimes life takes courage, and love needs to be nourished. All you need is time in order to let things flourish.

## Humidity

My mind is saturated, absolutely infatuated. In fact inflated in fascination, optic nerves lacerated in the image of her greatness. If by chance I should find a replacement or forsake it, be sure to have me incarcerated. She speaks slow, never regurgitated, the room reinvigorated, brought back to life like resuscitation. The vibrations of her voice reverberating like the sounds of liberation. She looks my way and I reciprocate it without faking. Still I'm waiting, the air filled with hesitation. Asking myself is it destiny or desecration; a lost man standing in a barren wasteland. Obliterated by her single glare, beauty foolish to compare. I'm illiterate to her stare, she looks through my like I'm barely there. So do I dare retreat, or am I just a light post along the street? Or maybe she's just a mirage in the city heat, transpired from all this humidity.

## Art of the Absent Minded

Mind it, I'm absent minded. I searched but couldn't find it. My sight is blinded. If you find it, confine it. Bind to a wooden board and grind. Flat line it, turn it to fine powder to do a line with. Because I don't need it, my skull is bleeding for seemingly no fucking reason. It was barely there so I never noticed it as it was leaving. I'm past the grieving, I never did. Got rid of the voices I skipped pebbles with. I'm a clever kid, and now I feel higher than Mount Everest. My fight method is being light headed, heavy footed and real reckless. Senseless in the battle field, a pen's the only thing I wield. It would be something if I could really feel, but none of this is really real.

## Crack

She had eyes like a pair of rare marbles. The kind I would have to work extra hard to win, carry around in my leather pouch the playground, all proud of myself. She had diamonds for pupils, no more carats than to compromise her genuine beauty. Satin sheets for hair and ceramic skin painted the slightest shade of caramel. Her words were just as sweet. Her velvet laughter like decadent crack for a fiend hungry to live again. She's pure-grade. Her flawlessness is perhaps her greatest flaw. Yet, I suffer the inability to completely fathom that I cannot acquire her. At least not so morally. Thus, withdrawal.

## Runout

Tranquilize this pain for me, haunting me so painfully. You came for me, disdainfully. Shamefully, though I tried to keep you away from me. Why would you take the blame for me? It's a mark of bravery for you to be saving me. No, you should run away from me. We're running through land mines so crazily, history on repeat. I say none of it is phasing me, but you beg to disagree. I'm several degrees below zero even in the summer breeze. I'll freeze before you ever get to reach out to me. I've sunk myself in the deep depths of the ocean. Frankly, because I've run out of all emotion.

## Limerence

A break in the tranquil, a ripple across my calm surface. Her beauty is like blasphemy. Because until now men only worshiped models. Idols with forcefully sculpted attractiveness. Her mind is an insolvable labyrinth, complete with both secrets and sorrow. The way she moves gives me motion sickness, because she possesses the eloquent grace of a summer breeze. Gentle. Yet so violent in bare presence like staring wide eyed at the sun during mid day. I'm stunned. And I need to ask her what she sees in me, if anything. And if that something is nothing, is nothing still something to her? Because that would be good enough for me. She's innocence if I ever saw it, in a crazy world mixed with lovers and dreamers and others mistaking emotions for erotica. But really, maybe we're both lost, just looking at each other wondering if the other knows the way home.

## Clusterfuck

Man or menace, evacuate all tenants. This cat is serving nine life sentences, no need to mention it, the judge would never lessen it. Because he left a bad impression, so that's the end of discussion, kid. Said you never know until you try, and so he tried it. And now he's drowning in silence, still racking up the mileage. Contemplation of coke up his sinus, he's so down to try it. Get lost in the high, leave his life right behind it. Blinded, the drugs are like time, liquid space, and her eyes are like diamonds. He's making idols like Simon, models with no hymens. Lost his mind when he graduated from grinding, and ever since then he could never find it. Because I trusted crazy hoes, but I truly cherished her. Always there when no one else would take care of her. Was the type to sit there and stare at her, but now such a loose character. It's a shame, to let all that go to waste. Lucifer fallen down from grace, angels wiped the smile right off his face. Big mistake; Hell would be a trip, he'd be sure to give a taste. He'll replace the gates of Heaven with a portrait of her face. Spending time on women that spend dollars on their waist, fabrics and the lace. Makeup to conceal imperfections and the frayed. Say to Azrael that Death is to be delayed, but Fate is never late. Faith has never failed, and Love isn't always great. Perfection is subjective, attention often neglected. A quarter mile of introspection could take him through depression. Handcuffs, stand up. Line up, man up. Jail cell, no bail. Trial and error, it ends here.

## KidxIsh

We're not new to this. If I'm an atom you're the nucleus. If I'm malnourished, you're the nutrients. Vitamins, now my life is brighter than it used to be. Okay, maybe this is new to me. I don't know what brought you to me. I'm not complaining, just saying things like this don't happen usually. We grew to be better people, good and evil, still as equals. If you're the feature, you're still the sequel. Like any plot we have our dark days filled with haze. Like stuck between a rock and a hard place, but it's okay. That's just the way life is, like it or dislike it. Just like sunshine and lightning, we have happiness and we have crisis. Time with you is priceless, a line with you is enlightening. But when the butterflies come around, trust me it's frightening.

## Alleys

The memory of you lingers like the glow from a lone street light. On in the day, on in the night. Unneeded, but there just because. Not because it has to be, but because sometimes the labor in such a task is futile. So I guess you'll always be here. Either to light the back alleys of my thoughts, or cast more shadows upon the weathered walls. You are welcome here, to come as you are.

## A Life of Substance and Sustenance
*For Omeo*

Appreciate all little things. Acknowledge and learn to appreciate the smallest of victories, such as waking up in the morning. You may have been fortunate to do so, but some others may not have been. Tomorrow, someone else might not be as fortunate. Plan ahead only for as far as you can walk in a single day. If you keep waiting on tomorrow you might never get the chance to live a day in your life. Breathe. Tell yourself you are beautiful, believe it. Then tell someone else. Learn to use your words. Make peace with yourself.

Wash, rinse and repeat for as many times as required.

## Particle Perfection

Pardon my aggression, it comes with the depression of suppressing emotions and second guessing. Myself, I never learn my lesson, I've been feeling lesser than the culprits of nine-eleven. Isn't that something? Fly a plane into my brain and put an end to all this stressing. I'm tired of recollecting, I get the message. I'll never be good enough, at best I'll come second. Particle perfection, the part of me you neglect so I'll never be your selection. Staring at my reflection, upon further inspection I realize I only craved your attention. Too late now, my feelings have been succeeded by emptiness. Those with smiles on their faces, I envy them. I was chasing a Kodak moment, dreaming and hoping I can keep it golden. But there's no point when I can barely hold it. I'm freezing and it's summer, it's a bummer, I could love her but not as lovers. Halfway to perfection, regret heard in my stutter.

## Counting Raindrops

### I

November rain, remembering past pain, feeling it creeping up like back pain. The same name etched into the back of my brain, story set in the past tense. She is in the past participle, memories continue to haunt and ridicule. And now I'm so cynical, I can't believe I flipped her reciprocals. And now it's tinted shades and a whole lot of praise. Saying goodbye to nightmares and hello to the glory days. I feel the bass pumping in my system and rattling the glass. Running laps but I'm not running back. Counting November raindrops, they say the coldest in the season. Plus this year winter is supposed to be freezing. I'm finally breathing, done with the grieving. Fuck a reason, if I'm leaving I'm leaving. And I've left, I just had to get this weight off my chest like losing a breast. I'm done losing my breath and thinking I was losing the best, because I just cheated death. Now my only focus is on paper, that's a new kind of stress. I'm dodging raindrops until this train stops. I mean, my thoughts – my mind's twisted in knots. Bring out the chalk, I feel a vein about to pop.

## Counting Raindrops

### II

I'm counting raindrops until my brain stops. No sane thoughts, I think I'll be stressing until a vein pops and I just stay in shock. Actually, fuck making sense of shit, I'd rather stay lost. Give me a shovel and a wooden box, weed paper and some eye drops. I remember when I told myself I wouldn't slip, and then I went and tripped over the same shit. Give me peace with a chrome piece with rubber grips, and don't you miss. I took a chance with the devil's ghost, shared a dance and fucked up my toes. So I'm lying here counting raindrops because I can hear the crows. The faint echo of death as the curtains close, the lights faded slow.

## Counting Raindrops

### III

Arms wide open, you running in like a sweeping tide. We had a moment there. As much as it soothes, why is it that rain also saddens? Or is it sadness that really soothes? It doesn't make any more sense when we question it. Nothing ever does. I try to keep count of all these drops of sadness but my ledger is always out of balance. I suppose there's no point in keeping track anymore when it's flowing over the brim.

**Shadows of Imaginary Friends**

## Moonshine Memories
*For Babu Uncle*

His vivacious laughter fills the room
A thunderous voice bouncing off the walls
He is animated, radiating; alive
But I know I am living in a memory
And when I wake, he will be gone again
The laughter will vanish, the thunder replaced with rain
But the memory of the gentle giant will always remain

*Naveed Khan*

## The Yearlong Season

Welcoming like a summer breeze
like a fond memory, displaced
Strong as the calm after a bad storm
Miserable, like the rain
as the loud cracks of thunder shatters hearts
The morning dew,
slippery and full of caution
Warm kisses
delicate like petals in the wind
This is a season that does not pass
transfixed in time
You are my past, present, future

## Halal

Keeping it halal isn't a trophy. Or something to show off like having gold teeth. It's beyond your own needs, it's for your own peace. Never hate the forbidden, you take in the same air they breathe. And it's not to change like the seasons, it's something you need to believe in. Not for the sake of #trends but with understanding for the reason. Like, what sense does it make to wear hijabs and skinny jeans? Tights and fitted means to look like models from the screens? Your mothers would scream, if they knew. Luckily they don't have a clue, especially what to do with you and your little sister. Say she's acting less Muslim and more like a Christian. What does that even mean though? Dad's whipping out the belt, his solution is simple. And none of it would have happened if you were never such a hypocrite. Never insult the faith you were born into, learn to be embracing it. Like, do you really need it, showing all that cleavage? Trying to live life halal but haram is what you're leading. What about the impressions that you're leaving? Young girls look up to you and see it, and that's what they believe. Practicing faith in the home, and flesh in the streets.

Halal is more than a word. Adhere to it before you claim to practice it.

## Memento Mori

*My mind's memento mori is the artificial photograph of me at the back of a bus. Artificial, because it's not real. Not real, not in being that it didn't happen, but in the sense that photographs themselves are artificial. Artificial images of an artificial world, artificial people, artificial moments. Printed onto paper, gloss or matte. A neat slice of time. Still artificial.*

*ar'ti'fi'cial – adj. contrived by art rather than nature.*

- - -

I think it's safe to say that I have spent the majority of my life riding on buses. I'm always in constant motion, going from one place to another for several different purposes. Even though I drive, the majority of my travels are done by bus.

I have actually had the privilege to meet certain individuals that have never ridden the bus, and if so have complained about the experience. They have complained about the wait, about the commute, about the people aboard them. These individuals have been mostly female.

I can't complain. I can't really say I love the bus, nor can I say I hate it. It has been, for me, the birthplace of many ideas, as well as problems. My usual seat is near the back by a window, head often propped against the glass and music drifting into my head through rubber coated wires. Made in China, of course.

I am a writer, perhaps in an exaggeration of the word. Maybe I'm just a person who writes rather than a writer per se. I am my own character in my head. He is for sure a writer, because I imagine him to be so. As I craft his story, he simultaneously crafts mine. This is how we correspond. We have a complicated relationship.

*I lost my mind here*, I tell him sometimes as we board the bus together. He frowns every time, perhaps in wonder. Or perhaps in contempt.

I have learned, painfully, that it is the spaces in between places that feel the loneliest. It is the travel from one place to another and the things in between that create voids. The roads, the cars, the people, the stop signs and traffic lights. That feeling creeps up on you. That feeling of knowing you're surrounded by people, but yet feel so alone. It wraps itself around you, strangling, convincing you that you really *are* alone. The beast has a name. Paranoia.

Then there's it's cousin, Panic!. It is the change in the wind, the staleness in the air, the sharp sting in your chest. Sweaty palms, racing mind, laboured breath. Pain. Panic.

I like to think that time stops when I ride the bus. But as I watch the scenery pass by I realize I am only but racing further into time, with time, and becoming one with it. I realize, sometimes, that time is the void between places. It is the force of attraction driving me closer to where I'm headed. It's fluidity scares me, invisibly inching down the crevices of my palms, threatening to finish me.

Time is nothing but liquid space.

The wait for the bus is tumultuous. It is one filled both with excitement and regret. It is sort of a love-hate phenomenon knowing the impending dangers of such a ride.

I must be an adrenaline junkie, for this is my daily rollercoaster ride. The doors open, and I pay $3.25 to lose my mind.

# B.I.T.C.H.

## Basic Idiotic Tendencies Cause Hemorrhages

I come correct, it's more than sex. Bitches with no intellect don't connect like no internet. Be direct but have self respect, treat yourself the best. It's good to be selective, drama bitches get neglected. Have a sense of self, introspective. Your mind, you have to honour it, everything in moderate. Be nothing less so others can respect my conglomerate. Bad bitches, there's a lot of them. In fact too many to run out of them. Never asked for a soap opera, I'll say it when I need it. All that TLC drama 365 days on repeat, shit. I don't know how they keep entertained, but they're not really to be blamed. Stuck in some kind of stage, perspectives all deranged. I don't know if it's their IQ's or how else to make any sense of it. But sometimes basic idiotic tendencies can cause brain hemorrhages.

Pow.

## B.I.T.C.H. II

## Because I Truly Cherished Her

Momma said to stay humble, don't fumble. Stay down to earth or watch the cookie crumble. Head up and feet forward so there's no way I can stumble. Welcome to the jungle, rumble man, rumble. Speak don't mumble, scream no stammering. Bad bitches hammering, thinking that they're glamorous. Posing with the cameras but really so amateur. I went there, came back, in truth it's just average. But you couldn't add up the fact that your intelligence is hazardous. Call me Lazarus, these words I'm spazzing with because mind is cancerous. I'll lacerate your wrists, masticate a bitch and spit her out into a ditch. Don't all Barbies come in bubblegum flavour? Drama like McDonald's, hard to digest like McLabour. I never savor the taste, I'm too wayward insane. Stay in your lane or I'll administer the pain. She sticks around like a bleach stain, please refrain. But a tiny little frame can still give crazy brains. I call her gravity because she always wants to bring me down. Her name is Prosperity but she never wants to see me wear the crown. She'd rather see me clown, happiest when I frown. Only a man when she's not around, so I pray she's out of town. Like, I can't believe I once thought she was a *Fareshta*. I only put up with it because I truly cherished her.

# B.I.T.C.H. III

## Because I Trusted Crazy Hoes

You swore you weren't as crazy as her. But I know when you hyperventilate, it isn't asthma. I'm not attacking you, matter of fact I wouldn't even look back at you. But the truth is, I'm accustomed to throwing a stab or two. You're not my ex but you still crossed the line. One of the only few to ever toy with my mind. Do me wrong again and I won't be the only one to feel the hurt. And for what it's worth, I'm likely to treat you how you deserve. I got a Louis Vuitton bullet with your name on it. But you're on that bullshit, so you should stay on it. I see you found sunshine, I should rain on it. But my hands are too precious to get your stains on 'em. That's why me and the bros never send a bitch *x* and *o*'s. I'm a cold motherfucker, because I trusted crazy hoes.

# B.I.T.C.H. IV

## Because I Totally Crushed Her

Such a trip. She wears her worth on her wrists. Tell me, was your soul worth the risk, or does your story have a twist in it? Here's a box, you can find my fucking fist in it. Don't touch that liquor, I mighta took a piss in it. I used my words, you wouldn't listen, you were too busy always twisting it. Don't question it, I just hope you ain't missing this. And if you did your ego wouldn't admit. Walk like a lady, bark like a bitch. But you're as cunning as you're stunning. Fellas call you hunny, you got their heartbeats drumming. But you only love money, and brands with bunnies. Hips shake like earthquakes, at first glance you're lovely. An innocent face with a delicate waist, elegant taste but deep down you got devilish ways. You'll take what I gave, break what I saved. Dismantle my face until my feelings have changed. Turn my blue skies into gray, fuck me over till I fade. Just being around you is a strain, we won't ever be the same. Just saying, we won't ever be sane. My friends saying I never should have touched her, let alone had loved her. I wish I didn't trust her, but I did, because I totally crushed her.

# B.I.T.C.H. V

## Before It Turned Completely Hell

Her beauty held me captive, what a tactic. Cupid's shooting arrows, I need some prophylactics. Or just some practice because I could never grasp it. How to avoid the danger of getting caught up in her labyrinth. I fell in love with her eyes, comparable to sunrise. I used to sigh, thinking if I were to die I'd just fall up into her arms – that's the sky. Heavenly enterprises, satanic disguises, especially through the angelic tears that she cried. I fell for it though, but boy was I surprised. In my mind I had captured every meticulous detail of this magnificent female, just like a work of art. From the shape of her nose, her beauty marks, the way her hair flowed, to the cut on her arm. I mean, I tried to put our names beside each other on paper, that's how strongly I craved her. I always tried to savor her like my favourite flavor. Tattoos and doing things taboo – we were glad to. But once you step on glass you're bound to take a step back; so we had to. Suddenly it was hellfire and the devil's choir. I wasn't tired, I wouldn't have it because I was on the pursuit of something higher. Nothing priestly, my genealogy is beastly. I slipped on grease but the situation wasn't so easy. So I told her to peep the reason I was losing sleep. I wasn't happy to just let it be, we needed changes that she couldn't see. Fuck depression, just hand me a Smith and Wesson. So I can Kurt Cobain my brains out and kill the second guessing. She still didn't get it, I guess she preferred me stressing. So I cocked the four-five and I aimed it at my chest. Took it off safety and listened to her breath. Fired it dead center and made sure there were no more feelings left. And I left, while she slept, before she could even tell. Everything was swell before it turned completely hell.

## Lullabies and Soliloquies

She sings lullabies, I write soliloquies. She says she feels for me, but I don't need her sympathy. Cry me a symphony. And say hi to him for me. She used to sing me to sleep, but now her tears keep me awake. Like that one nightmare that I dreamed, and now everything's starting to break. This is the part when things fall apart. So many broken hearts and a whole lot of scars. Sincerity smeared on the windshield. Only fear lives here, nothing else has been real. Pour a glass of liberty, get a taste of how sins feel. Roll the clip, next reel, that heart was a real steal. And my iron will is made with real steel, but her sex appeal makes my skin peel. You ever kissed but hated the aftertaste? Smoke on your lips during a masquerade. Holding her hips while the masks parade. She's sucking your dick and you blast her face. Grab her waist, saying you'll never give her away. But you never cared for her shame. Don't know her story so you ignore her pain. Prefer your hands clean but you'd let hers stain.

## Her Daily Wardrobe

She wears imagination as a crown and her body is draped in her dreams. She wears ambitions on her wrist, and hope stitched in every seam. She wears the shades of a bright future on her eyes, tones of kindness in her smile. She is heightened by heels of wisdom; she'll work only for happiness until she retires.

## Winter in July

Sometimes I'm not scared, I'm terrified. Terrified to the point where I'm petrified. Petrified as in paralyzed. Like staring deep into her eyes like an abyss of lies. Lies, like her true colours in disguise. More guys than I realized have been between her thighs. Too much between the lines for me read. The truth covered up too well for me to see. Anguish on repeat. Torn seams, broken dreams. Unleash the beast, and the demons inside of me. All these reside in me and her insecurities rely on me. She cries to me, says that we should try. But now it's gray skies, welcome to winter in July.

## Immaculate

She possess aesthetics beyond praise. Needless to say, her profound beauty left me speechless and amazed. Imprinted in my brain and left me in a daze. For days, I've been trying to catch her gaze. Because one look into her eyes takes me to a better place. She carries the warmth of the sun's rays. She's the one by whom I want my sons raised. She's got the touch of heaven's grace. She's like sunshine in the rain, acetaminophen for the pain. Innocent as a babe, strutting in her tiny frame. But despite what I have to say, she'll never look this way.

Thus, my feelings for her in vain.

## Welcome

Even doormats have more dignity, in that they at least get laundered. My welcome sign may be faded and worn but it's enough for you to make out. Certainly, it is enough for you to make yourself home for as long as you please. Knowingly or unknowingly, you'll prove yourself successful in transforming me from what I once was. Just like all those before you have. Before you leave, you'll wipe your feet on me one last time. Ensuring yourself above all others that you are well on your way. And if you are to return to this abode, you will do it all again, with no shame or regard.

But I swear, even doormats have more dignity. Because for me, I can't wash your prints off from my skin.

## Academia of U

I want to study you. I want to study your smile and every degree of your frown. And discover the ways I can turn it back upside down. I want to learn the things that make you tick, the things that make you flip. I want to read your lips and finish your sentences before you even say them. There's only one language I want to learn, and that's your body language. That is, the language your body speaks to me, so intimately, and I intently listen. Content with every lesson it teaches me. And I talk back, I ask questions. Demonstration, please! I'm taking note of the way you walk, the way you sway. The way the wind can't touch you, observing how heads turn your way and dense crowds part like Moses and the sea. And you see, I want to study your curves; the road between your teeth and your toes, every inch of flesh. I want to become familiar with your taste, and the shape of your waist, and the places I can rest my hands when they become too "tired" when out in public. Where I can wrap them safe, in embrace and warmth and have the peace of mind to know that they're in good care. I want to analyze every salty tear drop that falls from your eyes and trace them back to their origins. See, I can construct a complete descriptive course syllabus entirely on you, with an entire chapter dedicated to your mind alone. I want to associate with your mind and befriend your every solitary thought. In other words, I want to know you. All of you. Every last biological cell in your body. I don't need a textbook, all I need is you. Right in front of me ready to teach. Because I'm ready to learn. I'm ready to absorb you, like a sponge does liquid. I'm ready to embark on an academic journey solely on your being.

## Ill-Fated

I'm ill-fated, life's terrible demonstration. Curse my concentration, karma's condemnation. My mind is pacing, desecration. The dedication I once had now steady wasting in my cranium. Put me in an *insanium*, asylum. I'm like Odysseus feeling the wrath of Poseidon. I feel the heat like Hades, I'm underground like Osiris. It's such a crisis, I don't like this but like always I'll fight it.

Bring it on.

## Role Reversal: An Abusive Relationship

My addiction to your thighs got me ripped up deep inside. So accustomed to your lies, I'm expectant so I expect them; so I am not surprised. I wonder if I ever cross your mind or if you're still focused on other guys. I'm fine, I'm fine, and you're the number after nine. I love the flaws in your design, though I know you hate all of mine. All in time. Your beauty's so divine that it in itself should be a crime. Waiting for you to cross the line so I can punish your spine. I mean, give it to you from behind. I mean, let you suck it dry. I mean, wait, fuck it never mind. I seen that look before in your eyes, it left me traumatized. You abuse me, vandalize, and you'll see to my demise. It's like, every night I die looking up at the night sky. But I never seem to mind, as long as it keeps you high. But you've never seen the tears so you'll never know I cry. And you never pay attention, so you'll never know I tried.

## S.E.E.K.

### Search, Explore & Expand Knowledge

They say I'm overly ambitious, I say I'm just a victim of the capitalistic system that we live in. Project living and the projected profits they've envisioned. Speak out but they never listen, only concerned on divides between the Muslim, Jewish and Christian. But I ask you what's the difference? Hell, I must be tripping. Diamonds and jewels, they glisten. The rich are champagne-sipping, while I'm sitting here in class trying to work my way to first class. Wondering when my time comes, will it last or will I just let it pass? Living slow or living fast, concepts too far for me to grasp, because I'm trapped. Looking at the world through the glass, with pins stuck in my back. In school what do they really teach because the truth that we seek is too far to really reach. It's been whited out with bleach, so it's lost and now we're weak. The words I speak are expressed through gritted teeth. We're so consumed in grief they try to keep us asleep. The slippery slope is steep, the bottom is pretty deep. Make reality out of dreams and turn blues into greens. Preach.

## The Man Who Woke Up to His Face

He must have been dreaming. Couldn't remember the events from the previous evening. That party he can't even recall having leaving. The sex was steamy, but now he's feeling like he's freezing. He's trying to rid of his demons, so he takes another swing of the bottle by his bed. He's trying to find his meaning, but his feelings seem to keep fucking with his head.

He gets up and goes to the sink, there he dropped his drink. Looked into the mirror and he could hardly blink. He went to sleep as him, woke up as some else. His hands shaking, can hardly breathe and he can't call for any help. He doesn't recognize the man in the mirror, who he was supposed to be. It couldn't be any more unclear, if he told someone, would they believe? He took a closer look to see if he could recall. But the reflection looking back looked nothing like him at all.

His eyes were worn and red, filled with fear and doubt. His lips parched and swollen and had a cut inside his mouth. He called his best friend to see if she was free and could come up. But she picked up, didn't recognize his voice and so she hung up. He stood there in disbelief, through gritted teeth and threw the phone at the 60-inch LCD TV. Took another look at the mirror, then took his fists and broke it to bits in all his grief. He told himself it was a trick, that he needed to get a grip. Tried scratching at his face, around his ears, under his chin and by his lips. Thought maybe this face was just a mask and he could come out of it. Clawed at his face some more but only to cause damages. Started at his eyeballs, then proceeded punching his jaws.

But it wouldn't come off.

So he paused, went to the kitchen and pulled a knife from the drawers. Ran the blade right across his forehead, screaming in agony. Still he continued and bled, regrets he didn't have any. Then he dropped the knife and clawed once more to no success. Picked up the knife again and ran it across the parts of his face he had left. His eyes bled, mixed with salty tears and it hurt to scream. His lips were mangled and his tongue was split right in between.

He bled to his death on the bathroom floor without a face to identify. He died trying to find his face because he'd been living a lie. Call it fate, because when you stray you always have to compensate. There was no mistake, that morning he woke up to his own face.

## Shadows of Imaginary Friends

I

Puffing smoke with a bloody nose. But nobody knows that my body froze right before the very last blow. Heavy chest, feeling so morose for leaving him comatose in the rain, overdosed on the pain, killers are so deranged. But my fists are quick to fly, and I'm not satisfied until that bitch dies; I've changed. From a moment of being hotheaded, blood flowing like hot lead; poisonous and there's no avoiding it, like the doc said I've only got a couple days. I'm dazed, telling god I want to change a couple ways but I tread only deeper this maze. Amazed at the things revealed by perspective, things gone neglected but I've got no time to even regret them. Barely grazed my sense of self in contempt and lack of praise. In a lack of a better phrase, I was raised with good intentions all until I strayed. It never fazed me so I stayed off the narrow path, supposedly headed to grace. I found it strange. So I headed to another place, with the shadows of imaginary friends leading the way.

## Shadows of Imaginary Friends

## II

Led astray again through back lands with no back glance, backhands in rage. Fallen out of grace and nothing will ever be the same. So they say. The darkness can't be swayed and the demons can't be slain. Tread through uncertainty and sleep when you're awake. Fear is your master, hope is a snowflake. Collect wine from the river and make water from grapes. Insane. But fragility is a cause for shame. Humility is a waste. You have nothing to be happy for, you've got nothing to gain. Your life is just a stain on a canvas, painted out of anguish. Until you're forgotten and you're vanquished, as insignificance as outlandish. A story cast with settings you're likely to be regretting. A legend worth forgetting. Labeled through fables wayward and feeble. You search for an equal but no mind is as evil. In fact, even your shadow spites you. Safe to say only imaginary friends want to be just like you.

*Spoken by the Shadows of Doubt.*

## Shadows of Imaginary Friends

### III

The voices will say you have choices to make. Make sure you don't break, let alone make a mistake. The shadows of imaginary friends are there to lead you astray. Then leave you, afraid, far and desolate. Blue skies will turn to gray, happiness will fade. But doubt is the death of all things would-be great. Shadows rule over like pharaohs. Where sin is measured in kilos, regret imported in barrels. Welcome to the Kingdom of Doom.

Should you escape here, you will have found the Light. Should you stay, you might as well have never lived.

## Shadows of Imaginary Friends

## IV

Blithe, just breathe. Fly, you're free. Cry, you're weak. Hide, they'll see. Lie, or lead. Stay alive, or leave. Abide, or bleed. Smile, or sleep.

Because we are not your enemies, we are just your symmetry. Willfully or sinfully, we love you like a simile. Join us on the other side, where pain and joy are caramelized. In slow motion, all your dreams emphasized.

*We, are your friends.*
*We-are-your-friends.*
*Weareyourfriends.*
*Friendsfriends*
*friends*

*Come with us.*
*We are not your enemy.*
*We are just your symmetry.*

## Shadows of Imaginary Friends

## V / Dream Things

Keep your friends close, enemies closer. They're all a bunch of posers, pictures for the posters. They're like shoes, loafers, but shit I ain't lazy boy, I'm not your motherfucking sofa. I'm not your coaster, you need a new outlet for your toasters. Not even worth a cold shoulder, my fury's enough to smolder you. Quit acting your shoe size, fool, how old are you? You don't understand me but I'm standing over you. In fact, I'm just over you. Underestimate, but my respect from you is overdue. So you're bound to pay a fee, but the pain I administer is given to you for free. Agree to disagree, bleed through gritted teeth. You can cancel all my cards, take away my keys. Shadows of discomfort and dis-ease, but see I'm good with just my dreams.

*

## Dream Things

Sometimes, I struggle to distinguish Dream Things from Real Things. The two become so intertwined that setting certain things apart proves to be a challenge. Sometimes I'll live a moment twice, not sure if I had either dreamt it before or had experienced it consciously. Then there always certain things that I can swear are real, or may have been, but I later come to discover otherwise. Then there are the realities that can almost be passed as nightmares, and vice versa. Dream Things fill every crevice of my mind at times, replacing Real Things even in my conscious state. To the point, at times, when Real Things can hold a conversation and even shake my hand or go for walks. My physical me is met with my metaphysical me, both trying to make peace over the disparity of what's Real and what's a Dream. They say this is when the line has blurred. *What Line?*

## Primal Earth

This place is really strange, is this what Alice called Wonderland? Or have I always been here, I've always kind of wondered, damn. All I feel is thunder and lightning, these people are frightening. Chaos and disorder, conflict and fighting. Massacre and destruction, masses of corruption. Hunger is frequent and greed is triumphant. Nations in divide with hatred in their eyes. History repeats itself so you can count on the demise. Capitalism and greed, fund wars but refuse to feed. Blood for oil is the only reasoning you need. The weak cannot survive, the rich will never die. Inject them with AIDS and they'll still find a way to stay alive.

\*

How do we strive for normalcy, justice, and goodness in a world where violence and negativity have become the norm? Societal values are slowly decaying. Civilization is a broken system. We act more on impulse than we do through considered rationale. We, collectively as a people and species, are returning to our primal ways. Arguably, we may have always been this primitive as beings, however today, in this day and age these traits have become predominantly noticeable. Take a look around you, reflect, on yourself and others.

Is our ultimate fate of self-extinction inevitable?

## Documenting Rage

It's getting increasingly harder to contain myself. Once the rage takes over, I have a hard time seeing and thinking clearly. I'll spend most of my energy trying to hold back tears and fight the need to hit or break something.

*Crying is defined as "a complex secretomotor phenomenon characterized by the shedding of tears from the lacrimal apparatus, without irritation of the ocular structures." The medical term is to lacrimate. Is it supposed to hurt this much though?*

The dark bruises on my knuckles can tell a lot of stories. They have healed now, for the most part. A lot of skin was missing at given times, usually from punch brick walls. Not a good idea at all.

*Heavy breathing. If I'm breathing at all. I forget to breathe in times like these. My eyes burn.*

If I close my eyes, I feel myself getting up and flailing my limbs at either something or someone around me. If I keep my eyes open, I'll be frantically looking for that something or someone.

*Some holes are irreparable. They wouldn't be, but I make them so.*

I don't know what it is. I think it might be a sudden rise in my blood pressure that's causing my neck and shoulders to sear with pain.

*I don't want to think right now.*

This is just rage, I tell myself. Just an episode of anger. It can always be worse. And I really don't want to experience that again.

*Breathe.*

I'm going to count ten deep breaths.

**One.** *This really fucking hurts.*

I don't know why I'm doing this. This is so futile.

**Two.** *I hate feeling powerless.*

I can't feel like I'm losing control. Not now. Not ever.

**Three.** *My eyes are watering even more.*

**Four.** *Fuck you.*

OSAP. Die. Now.

**Five.** *Shit.*

No.

**Six.**

Lacrimating.

**Seven.**

I'll be fine.

**Eight.**

Okay. Okay.

**Nine.**

**Ten.**

*It's over.*

## Impressions

Suddenly, something just impressed me.

"You know why this so exciting?" I couldn't help but grin.

"Why?"

"Because for the first time in a long time, I'm impressed." It was true.

Only because I couldn't find any immediate flaws, or any reasons to dismiss her. The way I had become at a certain point in my life was particularly bitter, but of course with reason. She was a paradox, something strange. She didn't fit the common description at all. In fact, there wasn't one description to attach to her. Whereas before I would be quick to attach a label or apply a stereotype, she fit none. At least not very easily.

"I can't find anything wrong with her," I laughed, seemingly joking but not at all. "And believe me, I'm being critical. It's not like I'm trying not to find anything, I'm shocked at the fact that I can't."

"Either you're a fool, or you really like this girl," he said.

"Or maybe both."

I had become an expert in finding things I don't like in women at that point. I always knew the first places to look, as well. The common reserves were empty, free of stain.

"I don't get it," I steadily complained. "What's up with this girl?"

My friends just laughed. I chimed along.

I became obsessed in finding a flaw. Any flaw. An unattractive beauty mark, a bruise, a pimple, an orphan freckle. Anything to make me dislike the smallest bit of her, but the more I tried the increasingly more difficult the task became.

"I give up," I declared one evening at our usual circle.

"End of the pursuit already?" asked one of the boys.

"No, the pursuit just began. I give up on trying to find something about her I don't like."

Laughter, heads shaking. Relief.

## Rebirth

Jeans so saturated. Sedated, I was once infatuated. My heart, in fact you ate it. Constant fluctuation, fall from grace or fall from greatness as my interest elevated. Far from waiting. Heartbeat was decimated, estimated three days to live and I never made it. Gone again and then reincarnated, resuscitated. And though I hate it I take it as a lesson, so now I'm educated. Opinionated, peace in self-meditation and now I'm awake and I can put it all in my resume. The struggle of yesterday is just another step to greatness.

## A .45 Love Letter

~~she's the reason why i'm alive~~
she is bane of my existence

~~i'll do anything for her~~
she deserves nothing from me

~~she's an angel~~
she's the devil

~~i'll always protect her~~
i'll kill her

~~a dream~~
a nightmare

~~i cant live without her~~
i cant fucking stand her

~~i love her~~
i hate her

## Synthetic Happiness

I tell her that money can't buy happiness, she's telling me that yes it can. She shows me her heels and designer purses; I don't think she understands. Rings on her hand, it's like she's in a trance. Material demands, it's a common trend but I refuse to stamp myself with brands.

I'm happy the way I am.

## It's Only Beautiful Because It's Over

I don't want the title, I just want the content. Put it all in context, because you and I are still a misunderstood concept. Taunted but I used to flaunt it, don't get why the feeling isn't gone yet. It's like these memories are haunted. I'm lost, but fuck Google Maps. How to heal a heartbreak, you could never Google that. Words said, we could never take them back. But I'll argue with you all night just to make it last. You say, "Don't make me laugh," always trying to make me feel like crap. Okay, have it your way, it's already gone too far for us to grasp. Simply put, we'll never make it back. Because sometimes there are obstacles that you just can't make it past. Together we were music and now it's time to change the track. Whatever happened, happened, and it's best to leave it just like that.

## The Idea That Killed
### *For Ehsan S.*

"Have you ever been in love with an idea?"

Not love simply as admiration for but something profoundly more. An idea as vivid as a dream; something so engaging that you begin to need it, crave it, as much as you crave to breathe. It slowly becomes a part of you, or the need for it at least. For you crave to give its abstract nature some life, some kind of tangibility. *A taste.* It is your plethora of goodness, while not necessarily being all that good at all. The *idea of* becomes, in a dark and twisted way, a part of you entirely. Its presence and mere existence resonating throughout the corridors of your life.

Intangible, yet so lovely; you breathe an immortal soul into the idea. Place it on a pedestal higher than yourself or any other being. "So close," you'll say, "so close." So close to achieving that dream. *So close, but yet so far.*

But eventually, it will slip away. The pedestal does not in itself ascend before you, but rather you sink in despair in the wake of a strange realization. The realization that this *thing* will never be as you envision it to be. And what calamity you've caused by placing it higher than you can ever reach for yourself.

It's alive in a lifeless form. Taunting you, because you could never achieve it. An idea that shines brighter than all others, but devious like none. Your interpretations of the perfect imperfection, a masterpiece composed solely of thoughts and memories and dreams. Resonating throughout the corridors of your life.

The idea has made friends with the echoes of ghosts and the shadows of doubt. You cannot run from it. That which you have nurtured and cared for with every ounce of your being has turned into a boiling cesspool of hate. *But, you can't help but love it still.* Because it's yours and only yours, and no matter what shape or form it takes, it will always remain beautiful.

That's when you come to accept that you no longer mind destruction at the wrath of the idea. It *was your* idea, after all.

*"Have you ever been in love with an idea?"*

I have.

## Pursuit of Permanence
*For Anne N.*

*"It's broken."*

*"No. It's just changing."*

*

My feet dragged behind me along the long stretch of road, dirt and gravel and rocks. Cars passed by on either side pretty quick. No sidewalks. I chose to refrain from listening to music; I was content with the sound of my own two feet shuffling along the ground. I always enjoyed walks because they helped to put things into perspective. A little perspective was perhaps just what I needed. In fact, I wished they sold perspective as little energy shots at gas stations and convenience stores.

Exhaustion had worn me out, and it wasn't from walking. It had worn me out far before then, before I had arrived there twelve hours previous and had nothing to do with the fact that I hadn't slept in forty-eight hours. This exhaustion was more associated with frustration, anger. The suppressed brand. The kind you don't want to shake or else to have it blow up in your face. The kind that hurt. I've always been like that.

Late for work. To top it off, no smokes.

I hated smoking. Having vowed to quit so many times over, I never really did. Perhaps it was the mind set to quit that always prevented me from really doing so. What I did know was the reason why I smoked. It was because I always hated change.

Permanence was something I always sought after. Assurance and certainty; I craved for a taste of such things, in all things. I wanted to know that I could wake up every morning and find things exactly as I remembered them to be when I left them. It never happened.

Maybe it was because everything had always changed so fast and so suddenly that I could never once keep up. Maybe. I didn't know. My kid self was strapped onto a roller coaster ride at the age of only six or seven and that's how it had been ever since.

"I can't recall my childhood."

Growing up too fast had its consequences. Quite overly mature in some aspects and childish in others where I shouldn't be. Turned myself out to be a clown, but I preferred magicians instead. Magicians had a sort of elegance to their appearance. Clowns just always seemed straight out miserable to me. It worked I guess, because I always pictured life as a circus. Everyone had a role to play, everyone was a character, an eccentric, a freak or a weirdo. The magician stuck out to me, but in imagining myself as a character I had become the magician in clown shoes. It made no sense, but things rarely do when you're growing up.

Things never really do, actually. We just assign universally accepted values to things that otherwise have none. The colour red could have been called purple and people would have associated its emotions and semblances as purple. "Red" in itself was manmade and given a universal interpretation.

I sometimes wondered the same way about god.

In my quest for keeping things as much as I could, I seemed to have really lost myself. Smoking was perhaps an assurance that one thing would remain the same even though if all others changed. Perhaps like an anchor for my sanity.

Though running out of breath along the gravel path proved to me that I needed to give that up too. For the sake of my health at least. To think I once used to be athletic.

I missed running.

"Everything with a beginning has an end." I had always heard that and agreed with it but never really accepted it for myself. Instead I tried to fight the fact and search for something that wouldn't end. But it was quite contradictory that a cigarette would always burn out. Though I could spark another, the previous one would never be.

Perspective.

I realized that I was changing. Everything around me was changing too, always in constant motion. But for the first time I started to accept that I was, in fact, changing with everything else, and willingly so. The mechanics of my life were taking new shapes and forms, directing me towards a new path, much like the gravel path I walked. A path of perspective.

The realization occurred to me then that everything and everyone around me were a part of my safety net. A comfort zone that I created but needed to suddenly break free from. I had caged myself in and then grown too large to be contained much longer. Suffocation, if you may.

I learned that permanence tasted stale after a while. Things change, people change. Everyone has problems. Everyone has demons. Perspective helped me understand that. Also, that my pursuit of permanence was a pseudo state of satisfaction that I had created and trapped myself in. I wasted too much time.

Nothing is permanent.

## Physical

The attraction we've contracted at first contact has extracted our senses. With no further need to mention, we're eluded in the sexual tension. I could pretend not to feel it but there's no need for suppression. Besides, I believe in freedom of expression, and you're helping me release all this pent up aggression. I just ask that you don't regret it through all this shallow water that we're treading. If you dread it then forget it and I'll be sure to get the message. I know we come from brutal pasts and for that reason we've been numb since. So I guess what we're both looking for is just a little bit of substance.

Fragility of Fathers


Never there when we needed, no answer when we pleaded. Locked doors and profanity; as a kid I'd be concerned if my dad was mad at me. Then we grew to not give a fuck, just breaking stuff. Left the house when he finally had enough. They were supposed to be our role models, but I guess the pressures of the role got 'em. We had them in the spring and moved right into autumn. The void hurts to the point where they're better off forgotten. Momma says the apple never falls far from the tree. I know exactly what she means but I wish she wouldn't say that shit to me. But she ends up telling me I'm just like him. If he didn't do what he did that would have been a compliment. And I still don't get what it is that makes a dad so hard to deal with. As a kid he was a hero and grown up he's some next shit. Neglected, and disrespected. I had some shit to say but I thought "fuck it," and left it. So many conversations that I know we'll never have. And it hurts even more when they say, "You resemble your dad." Worse yet, all the words I could never take back. And the ego preventing me to even make attempt at that. Could I ever look you in the eye or spark a sense of pride? For you to hear me out for once and take my fucking side? Are you weak or misguided or were you not ready for this shit? Because I took people's advice and I tried it and I'm getting tired of it. The fact that we can't exchange a word without things blowing out of proportion. Photo albums show of different times, but you and mom should have got an abortion. If you can't take your responsibilities what gave you the idea that you could raise me? No, I get it – you're not cut out for me, I'm not fucking crazy. But I was just a fucking baby when you decided you'd betray me. The scene is over, the pictures hazy and even the heroic dad could never save me.

## Opacity

I used to love the feeling of everyone else around just fading away. It was like they weren't even there, and not for the reason of being alone, but for the reason of being left alone. It was always like time standing still, and us just being two of the only people left in motion. What mattered was directly in front of us. Nothing else was important. It was empowering in so many ways; a sense of empowerment laced with the eminent danger of vulnerability. In that moment, we left our defences open, because only we existed in the world we created. A city built with care, diligence, and ambitions. Perhaps we were overly ambitious. In being the only people there we assumed we were safe, but we never accounted for how vulnerable we were to one another. Winter dawned upon the city one morning, and it never left.

## A Field of Dead Flowers

I mean, it's not crazy what I'm trying to do
Trying to appreciate me but not depreciate you
Alleviate pain, bring light back to the room
Abbreviate my thoughts but everything ends with you
Believe me, this isn't the result of sudden clarity
I'm still blind, this is a heightened sense of sensibility
Through all the negativity, I'm taking on responsibility
For my actions, I've added all the fractions
Fractured the factor and although I hate decimals, I feel like
I'm a place holder
But believe me I have no right to hold this place
     – I'm colder
As the sun sets, painfully contracting, reverberating through
me
The world around me jovial but I'm everything gloomy
The sound of your voice resonates like a Mozart melody
     in a summer breeze
With a pinch of innocence, you sing beautifully
Open fields and blue skies, children flying kites
Our hearts dance in the sky among puffy white clouds,
     what a sight
What a feeling to feel, expand you into my lungs, I'm trying
to breathe
But all this stale carbon dioxide is really killing me
Softly but soundly, putting me to sleep
Plucking on my heart strings, you were everything real to me

I mean, it's crazy what I'm trying to do

## Born to Dysfunction

Chaos and calamity, sermons in profanity. Defamation in front of family, depravity. Apparently everyone's a celebrity, dreams of living lavishly. Spending money on things we don't need, especially when we don't have any. It's a travesty. I mean, tragedy. I mean, savagery. Prophecies and hypocrisies, pawns to monarchy and monopolies. How melancholy. Pussy is the new philosophy. Oral sex justified by Socrates: Tell her to give brains, for a life without knowledge is one lived improperly. Children of seduction, frequent to assumptions. Slaves to corruption, we were born to dysfunction.

## When Undressed

My objective is to make sure you don't object. To make you wet, dripping in thoughts of sex as I'm kissing you on your neck. My hands in places you didn't imagine they would be when you first met me. Or maybe you did, but whatever the case I'm sure you won't regret me. Don't get me wrong; I'm not this way because you let me. More like the fact that I sensed that you expect me. You rejected every other attempt, except me, and it looks like you're taking me in contently. The look on your face is sexy, serene beauty laced with the ecstasy of two bodies being intimately attached at the waist. I'm infinitely indebted to this feeling, but it's always well worth the wait. For feeling so weightless and transparent, your love for this moment and not for me is so apparent. We get dressed and part ways for clarity, but I'm honoured that we can share it. Because we might never be more than partners in bed, we have a strange relationship because it works only in our heads. It's an interesting experience, an educating excursion. What's unfortunate is that we probably know more about each other than the next person.

## You

Christened in your beauty, you're a cutie and you got no idea what you do to me. This is not normal but I'll take a beating like heavy duty. Is this the new me, or is this all just new to me? You're my cue to breathe, and you see right through me when there's nothing there to see. I'm burning up and I'd like to blame humidity. But I can't with all these feelings in my chest and this butterfly symphony. In sync to the percussion of your heartbeat, discussions of when two people apart meet. And don't mind me if I come off too strong. I know we haven't known each other long, so don't get me wrong. I'm hitting replay like my favourite song. Truth is, I think I liked you all along. You speak of deficits when I have a surplus of emotions from which we can both benefit. You, with the semblance of the moon, together we can try to make the best of it.

## Killing Your Ghost

I would gift wrap the globe,
put it at your toes
But now I'm so morose,
emotions comatose

You'd test my fuses till I blow,
so I headed for the door.
But baby we were close,
love on overdose.

This is the lifestyle that I chose,
your beauty's wilted like a rose.
And you cut me with your thorns,
with your jealousy and scorns.

I'm tired and I'm torn,
and you won't see me in the morning.
I hope nobody ever has to know or feel
how it's like to let go of something real

Wherever you are
I'm sure you'll know
Tonight, I'm killing your ghost

Wherever you are
I'm sure you'll see
What you'll never again mean to me

I'm slitting her throat
I hope you enjoy your own screams
I'm killing your ghost
So I hope you know just what this means

This is not an exercise
We could never compromise
I'm full from being fed all your lies
I'd go blind from looking into your eyes

I swear I thought I had a prize
But I never thought you'd make me cry
In the midst of building my enterprise
You brought me down to my demise

So I'm killing your ghost
I'm sure you know
And soon you'll see
What you'll never again mean to me

I'm slitting her throat
I hope you enjoy your own screams
I'm killing your ghost
So I hope you know just what this means

I'm so sick of staring at this ceiling
Done trying to figure out the meaning
You never tried to stop me from leaving
So me and myself is all that I believe in

Prepare a headstone for the heartless
I'm so gone, I'm in the darkest
Of places that I never thought I'd be
But at least I won't have you haunting me

I'm killing your ghost

## House of Mirrors

I love the way you look at me,
hate the way you judge me
And I want nothing from you,
I just want you to love me
Make me feel significant,
place nothing above me
I love the way you sound,
everything so lovely
I'm curious to know
what it is that you see in me
What do you see of me on the outside,
tell me what you believe
Because I know we all see
things a little differently
We're all seeds fallen
off from different trees
You really can't compare
like a metaphor or a simile
When it comes to people
there is no such thing as perfect symmetry
You and I are not the same,
no we will never be
That's what makes us
beautiful, not enemies
But perspectives can
be rather selective
Subjective, pertaining to
material and objective
In the end we're all human
so we're subject to error
Sometimes our eyes can play tricks
like a house of mirrors

## Serotonin Symphony

You feel the rush, it's building up. It's just enough for you to want to give a fuck. You're on the floor, don't need picking up. You don't need help, fuck a crutch. You were never out of touch, so you're never out of luck. Spend a couple bucks and then you're down to spill your guts. Confused between love and lust, you had too much but still not enough. You're tired of feeling like a speck of dust. Who do you trust?

Not yourself.

And now you're slowly winding down. Feet up in the clouds and about to touch the ground. It all comes back, you're somewhere lost downtown. Remembering how you sneaked out of the house, careful not to make a sound. You don't want the crown, you're just wishing you would drown. You're looking like a clown. Roaming aimless along the streets and it's time that you were found.

Stop choking. Keep hoping.

All you have to do is breathe. You're dying for some happiness, saying all you got is dreams. But you never once believed, in yourself and all the things that you could be. You're so appalled, because if you always look up you're bound to feel small. Learn to look below, cherish what you have and rejuvenate your soul.

You'll be fine.

## Quicksand

The feeling is foreign but familiar at the same time. Feeling stuck, hopeless, useless, all at once. The numb sensation sweeping over me like the slow tides of sleep lapping against the shores of my conscience. I can't feel a thing, but I feel everything. The metallic taste of defeat, that giant knot within my stomach that just won't untangle; they don't really help. It's true though, the more I struggle, the faster I sink. I'm idolizing failure, but chasing perfection.

You'll probably tell me that I should have known better.

I'll probably reply, that I do, but I'd much rather make some mistakes along the way.

## Earthquakes

Gentle tremors, to violent seismic reactions. The ground beneath my feet is fragile. So much, in fact, that sometimes I'm afraid to apply all of my weight. The danger of the mysterious and unknown versus the familiarity of calm and comfort. They are both equally attractive elements, but to choose one over the other poses to be increasingly difficult. I'm not quite sure if I would settle for the serenity of heaven over the tortures of hell. I've been afraid to feel, but if I feel, I fear being too accustomed to the point where I become numb to the sensation all together.

Maybe I prefer to stay afraid.

## Blanc

She says I got a way with words
I think I just get away with words
In a wayward way, I play with words
Just pray I never run out of words to say
The weight of the world weighs heavy on my soul
So I wait for the beat, catch some release then lose control
Gone is my senses, suddenly I'm senseless
Write her a new letter, grip tight before the pen slips
Walking down the same paths with less direction
All this bottled up aggression, she promises protection
But like always I'll refuse her, hoping not to lose her
She knows all my problems, she stays quiet while I abuse
I run to her when I need her and push her when I don't
Sometimes I think I should erase her
but I need her so I won't
I'm terrible, I'm a maniac,
I cut into her skin like a tree and axe
But still she fills in the gaps
for everything I lack
I can tell her that I love her,
but she stays quiet every time
Words only scratch the surface,
she can read between the lines

I'll be honest,
she's a light-skin goddess
But she's always simple,
she stays modest
You could say she's my savior,
when I'm down I crave her
That's why I'm in heaven
every time the pen touches the *paper*

## The Crawl

Noose around the neck, living cheque to cheque. He's out to gain respect, but to the world he's just a speck. Life's test, threw him in the projects. Potential prospect stuck with hooligans and thugs living lawless, and "fresh-to-deaf." He only bumped to the clef, compliments to the chef. Looking through the world through a prism while stuck inside a prison. So filled with determinism, you can't say he isn't. Never the chiseled individual out to make the female genitalia moist. He was the geeky little dude that got good grades in school, not all by choice. He was on the rise from the fall, he had no help at all. He wouldn't rest until success, so he accustomed himself to the crawl.

## Tears of a Sadist

His face is etched with permanent-marker-guilt. Hard to wash off. Even harder to hide, though he seldom finds the need to. It is a distinct look that is unmistakable, but often prematurely dismissed. An immaculately sinister smile reveals clear intent. Slaughter of innocence. Hurting himself more than he is others, but the thrill excites him. Inciting his schemes, fueling his motives. Giving birth to his fire. With eyes ablaze with passion, he's a magician. But he dons clown shoes.

He laughs only because he cries.

*Cheap Therapy*

*Inna Lillahi Wa Inna Illaihi Rajioon*

May the souls of the deceased rest in peace
In their respective beds six feet beneath
The surface, where sins are known to creep
No grudges shall they keep or be kept as they sleep
One with the earth and the dirt that forged us forth
Giving life to air, to the very breath that taught
Respected and revered in thoughts, remembered in mirth
In life we immerse but "We belong to Allah and to him we
return"

## Fair Trade?

We trade faith for fashion, wisdom for weed
Anything for flashing, glorify the grief
Put on a pair of glasses, ignore all the need
This is the generation? Lord, I can't believe
A battle lost without fighting, worse than retreat
Dance away the nights and spend days in greed
Inclined to believe, that we're the best of all the seeds
But we're still a couple germs just lost in the sea
Constant infatuation, with always being infatuated
Stupidity, logic and sensibility all evacuated
I was told to live like a tourist, like I'm just passing by
People are getting comfortable watching the time fly
But when it's time to fly, some stay firmly on the ground
Incapable of flight as their black hearts weigh them down
It's a truth of life, you have to earn your wings
You'll only learn the from the lessons the journey brings
So when you trade knowledge for ignorance, is it really
worth it?
If it's a fair trade for your soul, I welcome you to the circus

## Hate Harbor

moving bus in flames
fireball on the highway
shattered windows
imploded faces
exploded belief
mangled perspective

leave your thread
mark a spot
jog or not
light head, dead
blue is the only colour
that can make red

the sign
at hate harbour reads
welcome to *animonstrosity*
racial profiling
accepted here
kindness can
kindly leave

## In Motion

Only change is constant
and we are in constant motion
Moving towards destruction
or nothing
But nothing is still something
with another name
And a name is at times
all one has to live for
To live in the moment
or simply in motion
With the fluidity of time
or as time itself

## Bones

My mouth is numb from having tasted your pain. The touch of your fingertips has started to make my skin flake, sending shivers of bittersweet agony coursing down my spine. The sting of your glare continually overwhelms me with a kind of inexplicable grief; your eyes consume me whole. You're stripping the layers of my sanity and I've become too apathetic to even feel the slightest bit humiliated. You're sedated by misery, having perhaps mistaken it to be happiness. You're going nowhere in particular. And you're convinced to take me with you.

# Cheap Therapy

## Cheap Therapy

I've found a way to channel my anger in a way that is less destructive to property, however, perhaps a bit more destructive to other people and myself in ways that aren't always physical. It's something I can't always control. I've always been angry, I'll always be angry. I'll say things out of anger, not everything I'll actually ever mean but most of it. I guess if I didn't have words, I really would resort to physically hurting someone. Like punching someone in the face and busting their lip again. I've come a long way from uncontrollable angry fits to being able to stay generally composed throughout a situation now. But the anger always feels the same.

## Why, right?

When I speak, I feel as if I'm talking in another language. So I go either unheard or misunderstood. When I write, it's at least being accepted. I have only one audience, the paper, and it neither applauds nor approves. But that's okay. What is most important to me is the feeling that I get from finishing a piece. It is a sort of high for me. One that only lasts me about thirty seconds, but are my only few seconds of glory and utter happiness. Happiness, not because I wrote, but because I created something I can truly claim to be my own. That is why I write.

## Stripes

Elongate the fury
Stretching it's relentless wrath
Postpone Azrael's scheduled inspection
Inflicting imposition of conflicted interests
Parallel to perfection
Pitching fevers and prospective favors
Paracetamol for the parasitic
We could never have predicted
the degree of our destruction

Redemption.
Regret, rebuild, rinse and repeat.

## The Monster's Keeper

You are the monster's keeper. Gripping his reins, hopefully, tightly and within your sights. The little weapon feared by the few that never understood the love of the many. To witness and withstand the pitfalls and diggings -in and out of- graves and tombs. The burning down and destruction of cities and the sudden complete numbness. You're dancing with the devil's ghost. You are the monster's keeper.

## Pogs and Paper Bag Lunches

I want to lie awake in the nakedness of your mind. As your dreams of the moon shines through the blinds, in a world where we're not bound by time. I want to befriend your sorrows and ask them if they'd like to borrow a little bit of cheer. And so I promise you by tomorrow, you'll have absolutely nothing to fear. I want to know your thoughts like I know my way home. But I don't know either, so maybe that makes us both a little less alone. And I'd love to tell you how unafraid I really am, but I'll tell you when I really am. Because certain uncertainties scare me to the point where I fail to understand. But I guess it's all just another part of growing up. In the rush of it all, I hope we don't grow out of touch.

The novelties of this newly attained life offer us a strange sense of familiarity as compared to those of our childhood. But one thing is for certain, the ability to feel is truly a phenomenal thing.

## Definition:
### gray

(colour) you don't know loneliness until you're put into a room full of people and still feel completely solitary

syn: ghosts

## Cigarette at Sunrise

I'm out when the sky is just beginning to blossom
Casting its pink and orange hues against the clouds
The fire is warm, the one in the sky
    and the one between my fingers
But sadly I cannot feel either,
    but what I feel instead is emptiness
A shallow vessel of words and expired emotions
A container filled of nothing else but air
    as spirals of cancerous smoke devour my face
I'm trying to piece together a puzzle of a blank picture
There's no point in figuring out what it means,
    because it means nothing
But sometimes the mind can play tricks
    and show us things that aren't really there,
That never really was, and never really will be
The world will go on with its regular business,
    as it always does
But I feel like I've fallen behind
While standing in the same spot I've been standing
    for what seems an eternity
And internally, I'm trying to hold onto what's left
But tying up these loose ends will surely take some time
Who would have known that growing up meant growing old
Before I get the chance to actually be young
But I guess I'll always be a kid at heart
So I smoke, knowing I'm not guaranteed a breath tomorrow

Good morning.

## Clown Shoes

Every night he would recall the dark corridor outside his room. The shadows cast upon its walls, the muffled screams, the silhouette of a hand raising in the air and falling to its victim. He blocked out the rest. Because that's when he would close his eyes and cup his ears tightly with his palms.

Sweat.

It was a stark difference from the colour and cheer of the circus. But that was in the day, in the night, there was no colour and there was no cheer. There were only more dark corridors, like the ones from his childhood, and more shadows. Long silhouettes of men fornicating behind the living quarters off to a distance, the faint groans, the creaking of the wooden boards. It was a different sort of hell.

But it was home. It had always been home. Though there was no sense of welcoming or warmth to it, it put something over his head, so therefore it must be home.

Home wasn't so bad in the day time. It was only in the night and when he couldn't sleep, which was the case more than half the time usually. But the days were filled with life and excitement. Men who fornicated with men walked tight ropes and jumped through rings of fire and did gymnastics and rode around on unicycles. Everyone was happy. Especially the children.

He did it for the children. Because their smiles and laughter made him feel warm and accomplished. He felt it made up for all the bad, for all the running-away-from-home and setting-things-on-fire and "accidentally"-stabbing-mom's-boyfriend-in-the-hand-with-a-phillips-screwdriver.
He felt at peace with the children. More importantly, he felt important. Needed. He was a spectacle.

And a freak, some might even say.

He pulled rabbits and white doves out of his hat. Yards of coloured handkerchiefs, coins from behind children's ears (which they were allowed to keep) and even cut them up and put them back together. He could tell them which card they drew from a full deck -- without even looking! He could start fires in mid air with a single snap of his fingers and make anything disappear. He was out of this world! He caused awe, and he made their eyes sparkle with wonder and inspiration.

He only did it for that. To feel the energy of the children. To feel alive for about half hour to forty-five minutes at a time. He was quiet then. And when he wasn't performing magic, he'd be screaming, but he was still quiet then, too.

When his cheap tricks and routines weren't being performed for the children, it was his mind that pulled the cheap tricks and routines. Shadows and blood and water dripping and screams and fire. He hated the fire. But that's all he ever saw.

Everything was burning. The whole circus was on fire when he wasn't performing magic.

"Hey mister!" yelled one of the kids during his routine.

He couldn't hear him. He smiled as he set up the next trick, but in his mind he saw the violent flames of his childhood home.

"Hey mister magician!" yelled the little boy again. He caught his attention this time and stopped midway to look at the brown-haired child.

"Why are you wearing clown shoes?"

The children all began to take notice of the erroneous attire and all began to laugh rather violently.

The magician smiled, simply shrugged and carried on.

## Sensibilities

Your eyes stuttered when they spoke to me, but hopefully and irrevocably. And I was lost within them totally. Though astonished by their legibility, I would never question their credibility. I admire your sensibilities, especially the specificity of your ability to bring out the best in me. So whenever you're in the vicinity, all I feel is felicity.

## Freewriting

Head in a dark place. My thoughts are swirling, slow, thick, like smoke. Concealing me. Everything. Visibility restricted. Choke. Don't choke. Open a window. There are no windows in this room. Stupid. Yes there is. No. Shut up. Okay. Breathe. Just breathe. What's a nose? Fuck it. Fuck everything. No. Don't. Everything is too big to fuck at once. Maybe not. PhD. What the fuck. I can't do this. Yes I can. I lied. I really can't. I don't know why I'm trying. Or maybe I'm not trying hard enough. What is enough? What is? What? I don't know. Stop asking so many fucking questions. Fuck you too. Fuck you too. Fuck you too. I can't fall. We all fall. We all fail. I'm afraid to fail. Failure is the name of the shadow that haunts me every night. Creeping over me along these walls. Stay the fuck away from me. Don't fuck with me man. Don't fuck with me. I'll fuck you up real good son. Don't fuck with me. I'm sorry. I'm so sorry. I didn't mean to hurt you. I can't take the fucking sadness in your eyes. I can't stand it. I can't bear to endure another comparison. Stop. Please stop. Can't you be happy with me. Where the fuck am I. Ok head is spinning now. Okay. Okay. Breathe. Breathe. Fight it. Fight it. Why doubles? Why so serious? Joker. Arkham. Okay. Okay. Uhm. No. I'm sorry. I'm sorry I couldn't be what you wanted. I'm sorry. I'm not good enough. It's okay, maybe you'll be proud of me someday. I'm sorry. I can't do this right now. Stop.

The Traveler:

The Arrival


I swear when you came in, I felt the ground shake. And how I felt, somehow it all changed. A pretty face, in a small frame. It's like I've been looking for you, always. Something new, something I'm not used to. You said, "I can't choose you." I said, "I can't lose you." So I guess, it's just business as usual. I don't get what you're afraid of, I love you with no make up. I guess we're safe when there's nothing there to break up. So we're constantly making amends. Don't want it to end, so I had to settle with friends. I don't want to taste defeat. So we agreed to never make promises neither of us can keep. You say you came from far away, something like overseas. Saying how you came to stay, I guess we'll have to see.

The Traveler:

The Stay Pt. 1
*For Adam T.*

It's just you, me, and these faded white walls. Who sent you to me, when I was reduced to a crawl? I can't breathe, can't sleep. You put your arms around me and let our bodies do the talking and take away the grief. And then you say that you should leave. I say you don't, but you say please, let it be. Because you're not the one I want, you're the one I need. So I need you to just stay, and fill my void and greed. You understand, I can tell from the way you hold my hand. Your hurt, it's her, she's the one I've saved the words for, as planned. It's not right, I hate how the days have turned to gray. Okay, I'll fight to make her stay. It won't be right away, but she'll come around some day.

The Traveler:

The Stay Pt. 2

I've been too busy falling for you. I've been thinking this through, how one and one equals to two. Split from each other, and it still equals to two. Because I'd be in pieces if I were separated from you. I'm constantly left without a clue, made to clean a mess without a broom. So a me without a you, it's like night without the moon. Hair without a "do," a theatre without the troupe. Or a kid without a shoe, or..porn without the nude. You're essential, especially when you bring out my potential. According to your credentials, you knew my fall would be eventual. And for once, it doesn't hurt like I thought would. I been through a lot of bad, but I can tell that you're a lot of good. Have faith or call it fate, I hope it doesn't change. I know you travel a lot, but thanks for choosing to stay.

## The Traveler:

## The Departure / The Voicemail

I want back all my things, everything I ever gave to you. You shouldn't still wear that ring, but you're convinced you do. You're a bitch, it's confirmed, you'll never learn. You're out to scratch an itch, I hope you know you'll burn, you've been warned. I just want back all my shit, like all the time that I in-vested. All the roads and the dotted lines, and the useless memories that take up space in my mind. Words that were intertwined, inclined and in between individuals clearly blind. All you had to do was break my fall, but you chose to leave me at a crawl. I've befriended these cold walls and thanks to you I'm no longer afraid to fall. But don't you forget, I know how your story ends. I won't sugar coat, my dear, I'm not good at playing pretend.

*

## The Voicemail

You say you're traumatized. The pain is caramelized, slow and sticky like the sorrow in your momma's eyes. I've seen it before, once or twice, before the sun would rise and you'd be looking into mine. Let out a sigh, unknown for what for, but I knew deep inside you cried. Once loved, you're everything I despise, for your lust for my demise and your constant lies. To no surprise, you're a fucking shark. You saw me sinking so you took a bite out of my fucking heart. Don't ever leave another message after the beep, unless you want what's left of yours torn apart.

## The Suicide Bomber

Where I'm from the lights are always flickering
Nobody's listening, yeah here we go with this again
No water in the kitchen, no gas to light the stove
The lights are always out man, where's a soul to go
Oh, no bread and butter for the fam, how to break a man
You size him up with your eyes but you'll never understand
Speak ill, break his will to want to even carry on
Drink dirty tap water, the rich sip on Dom Pérignon
Art; contrasts of life, go well beyond abstract
And these colours will never mix - white is white, black is
black
There's nothing in between, no gray area is what I mean
Because as long as we live, difference is all we see
So what an opportunity to come to the land of opportunity
To be only faced with scrutiny, cultures dividing you and me
The clashes of classism and racism, sexism; discrimination
Of self, because all we discriminate is our selves
You, me, her and him, we and they
    What's the difference anyway?
Explain it to me, plain words for my kids to understand
Why they're looked at so different like a piece of contraband
Why does a turban make you a terrorist, a beard link you to
Al-Quida?
Islam never taught hatred, says to even spare the life of a
spider
Misinterpretation is the culprit, but you needed someone to
blame any way
But face it, we're all companions of fire – we'll burn in hell
soon any day
Cheap thrills like a whore, all that really matters nowadays is
to settle scores
It makes sense; the suicide bomber died because he had
nothing to live for

## Ecstasy

I wish I could capture the look of ecstasy on your face. But no images or worded descriptions could ever do justice to that single look of perfection. The arch of your immaculate brows, the sudden heaviness of your eyelids, the slight part of your lips, and your head tilted to your left shoulder. You emanate a rather dangerous kind of tension. The look of lust in your eyes sends violent jolts through my spine, awakening a more primitive, animalistic side of me that I had long since forgotten. I want to devour you. All of you.

## Every Pack is the Last Pack

I buy my friends in packs of twenty. Stories, I have plenty. They listen, and never seem to resent me. Thoughts of suicide, but they would never let me. I'm good until they're empty, every pack is the last pack, but goddamn they're so tempting. So they tempt me, and together we rewrite my ending. Twisted with overspending and looks from people condescending. But they don't understand; familiarity is the greatest comfort I could ever feel. My disparity lies in separating a dream from what is real. I'm sinking, trying to keep myself from thinking. Blinking, zoning in and out, wish I was drinking. My vision hazy, black and white, like I'm seeing zebra. I think I'm going crazy, so they promise me "We'll never leave ya." Okay, thanks, I believe you. I got stories to tell, so sadly I still kind of need you.

## Another Letter You'll Never Read

Maybe I don't know how to communicate, but shed some light on me, illuminate. What do you want from me? Reiterate. I know the path, but I choose not to walk it straight. I wasn't born left-handed, I'm sorry you won't ever understand. But your words always come back to me like a boomerang. I know you raised me right, but there's more to me. The one thing you instilled in me was the value of honesty. So I tell you honestly, you can't read my eyes like you did when I was a child. I learned to hide, and though it took a while, I learned it's far from telling a lie. It's just my way of never letting you know how much I die inside, whenever you compare or I fall beneath your condescending glare or the way you stare whenever you hear some lady's son went away to do their medical degree somewhere. Seriously? Is that all it takes to make me break? So let me ask you this, would you have thrown me away if you found out I was gay? I guess that's why respect turned to neglect, and my emotions patted down to cement. I'm a wreck. But believe me, I don't care for your discomfort or blatant retort. All I ever ask of you, is a little bit of support.

## This Placed

From the high pitched shrills
of the streets of Dhaka
Risking life on rollercoaster rickshaws
Rickety roads plagued with potholes
and political rallies
and the permanent mark of impoverishment
to the sophistication
of London's double-deckers
Carried on cluttered seats of a Boeing
economy class, of course
to the quick cabs of New York City
Displaced, still, to the run-down
thrift store beginnings of Montreal
Where the best commodity in
transportation was a stroller
No, a bike
"Je ne comprends pas"
Whisked to winter wonderland
Winnipeg was cold
Hyundai, a hatchback
-- used, of course
Snow bank winters
and sand bag summers
Train to Toronto
1990 Toyota Corolla, in red
(such an ugly car
but it got the job done,
it really did)
Kingston
Life in a motel, for a month
seemed like the epitome of childhood
The fish fingers
at the day care was
the best, by far

And the shopping carts were
race cars
Until one left a, Scar
– borough was foreign
It specialized in gossip
Twisted tongues and wrong turns
Etobicoke, a disaster
as innocence played amongst shadows
And violence became a best friend
Brampton, a wasteland
stretching for miles of nothing
But the stars are the brightest
here

## The Antihero

I am not myself. I am anybody but myself. I am everybody and nobody. They say nobody is perfect, I say nobody's nobody is perfect. But perfection is subjective. And perfection is nothing. Nothing is something with unfulfilled potential. Potential has no potency. It has no substance; just empty and insignificant. I am not myself. I am nobody, and no body's original, nor cliché. I just am, a being that ceases to be. The effort is painstaking. Murderous. If I drown, will I save me? No, I has to learn how to swim for himself. The main stream is diluted. All that water has made it shallow. I am not. Anything. Any thing can be cheap. Too loose, too free. I need a tighter noose. Myself. That is, two, but singular. Just me, without me. I is sinking. I am. I am not, my self.

## Fucked Up

There lies a strange, dark, and unexplained beauty in the state of being fucked up. And as fucked up as that sounds, it's going to get even more fucked up. I wonder, sometimes, in my little corner of the world, what it will be like to one day not be so fucked up. But then the most fucked up feeling dawns upon me. Not be fucked up? What the fuck does that even mean? I mean, how do I even begin to comprehend that? I think a part of me always wants to move past this fucked up stage in my life. But the realization strikes me now, that if one day I were to overcome being as fucked up as I am today, I would be fucking miserable. Everything would change. I would have figured it out. It would be the end of my discovery. It would be the end of me, as I know it. And now, believe me, I don't wish to be more fucked up, but I don't want to be not fucked up either. I don't want a fucking cure and I don't want anybody telling me why things are the way they are. Fuck you. I'm allowed to be fucked up. So let me be fucked up in my own fucking ways, because that's what makes me who I am.

## Sleep less, dreamer
*For Jaleel H.*

Simmering lights of the city skyline offer a cold slice of peace. It's a strange substance that seeps slowly but surely across heavy eyelids, teasing sleep, but squeezing out every last drop of sanity, and replacing it instead with violent subtleties. A less than simple soliloquy to the audience of myself substitutes as a lullaby as I enter a nightmarish dream sequence. This falling asleep is really the waking up again to the realities of my life.

# My Apologies

I'm deeply sorry for your loss, but maybe not sorry enough. I'm definitely not sorry enough to be able to compensate in any way or form. And I'm not sorry because I should be or have to be, but sorry because I genuinely want to be, and therefore am. I'm not sorry because it's expected of me to be by the teachings and practices of societal norms which, quite frankly, I could care less about at this point in my life. The mannerisms here have taught me to smile and shake hands when meeting people, but also to talk ill and plot against them when they are absent. The very system of values this society tries to uphold has no firm foundation, for it had been uprooted a long time ago. Where now it has become a norm to accept and not question, to follow instructions and never oppose, wonder, or even ask as to why. The way it works is to keep the general population stupid, so to be able to feed them with lies and instill false needs. Capitalism has become cheap. So I do apologize for the desensitized pricks you'll meet, the inconsistency and inefficiency of society. I apologize to you especially for the flawed education system. You came here on the promise of opportunity, and perhaps a bit of opulence, but all you ever got was the occasional offer of condolence. Such that I'm giving you now. But I really do apologize.

## Usually

Usually is such a strange word, but one we're so used to that we usually never notice. What is so common or customary about a thing that deems itself as the usual? And what defines common, or customary anyway? Usually is a loose word, often thrown over concepts with its ends trailing like baggy clothes. It is perhaps ambiguous at best, because its utterance has no signified mention of the last time the qualifying traits of usually occurred. Usually is a vague lie, sprinkled with a half-promise of truth. Usually has given wake to nations, or perhaps notions, of believers.

## As We Make Music

The quiet cadences of careful caress confirm our thoughts and emotions more than they suppress. Who would have known that touch had a unique rhythm of its own? I didn't, did you? But I'm not complaining because I love this view. Your semi-golden hue in the light of the sun in my room; my mind is blue. Blew. Blown. You're a goddess with the ability to give life to stone. The only thanks I'll ever take is the look of ecstasy painted on your face. Your muffled whispers as I muster both strength and precision, careful not to break *(brake)*. Your glow has started to pull on my soul. With each angelic moan, I lose a bit more control.

Music never sounded this good.

## Rearview Reminiscent
*For M.B.*

Intimacies and intricacies, in our heads we're celebrities. Or paper planes soaring in the breeze, the latter of the two blowing through the trees. The scatter of leaves, the wet sleeves and tattered knees. Battered, we bleed, is blood crimson or is it burgundy? Bicycle helmets in a burglary. Restock from the closet armory or perform cardboard surgery. Can words be physical? Can emotions be reciprocals? Growing up was so pivotal, but so unscrupulous, it's ridiculous. With the frivolous stimulus of the promiscuous. Infinite amounts of mischievous bouts and back when we thought we were invincible and limitless. We were gods, so ubiquitous, serendipitous and filled with fearlessness. We resisted submission, until we synthesized and synchronized, realized that we had to leave. You and I, we left our childhood back a couple streets.

## August 26

Tough luck, they say. Some people never get a break. They just get broke, not too far from broken, even. But never breaking even. Never even. Or just never. Opportunity had two legs and got lost. Mouths to feed means dreams to leave. Working class heroes with workplace affairs. Maybe they're tired of all work and no reward, not even a thank you. Thank you. Fatherhood is a thankless job, after all. Full-time tyrant, part-time dead. Asleep, anyway. The nearing sirens, domestic violence. Screams, severance, silence. All in that sequence. Rewind it, and play. Again. Again. This is a VHS cassette, no skipping chapters. You know how the story ends.

# Friction

Let me be your doctor and fill out your prescription, to a dose of bodily friction, legs numb in constriction. No reservations, no resistance, just perspiration, no restrictions. Lay back and allow me to crack your body's encryption. Let me christen your holy temple with my loaded piston. You're going to moan, I'm going to listen, especially to the choice of tone and vulgar diction. To uplift you is my mission, our tongues twisting, we mix in the sweet substance of our elixir. Sex with you is bliss, engulfed in the flames of a euphoric fix.

## Eyed in titties

Writing, merge in all
The offer of solutions still
render conflicts unresolved
Between breaths and
the breathtaking
A dose of absence
or absinthe
Casually, casualties
Cause and because
For before, forebode
The pauses in poetry or prose
like probably posterity
Calm before calamity
Clones, cataclysm, catacombs
A loan will leave you alone
Broken bro-kins
Love turned loath
Not In Pak
or Packed In
Chris kissed Jew
be Hind you?
Or Is Lamb?
Bengali Can
or Can Bengali?
Can, not
Canadian
   Eh?

## Way St.

I pray you're not wasting your words on me, like you would to a deity. I encourage you to think freely, really. Believe in me in practical amounts only, and let me know when I let you down. I warn you now, for if you are wasting words, choose the ones you want to dispose of within me carefully. Because I'll be forever recycling them and playing them back in my head, trying to match the initial honesty they contained coming from your lips. I hope I'm everything you see or say I am, because I would truly hate to be that much of a waste of words.

## Bits (and pieces)

He moved closer to her, reached for her hand and slipped the ring on her finger (like he practiced), all the while wearing an almost apologetic face for having done so. He could feel cold sweat beginning to creep down the back of his legs and calves (he hated that). He personally preferred drowning as opposed to feeling the anxiety he felt. He looked scared (of her words), she looked bewildered (because of his actions). Their eyes met briefly, but something was wrong (everything was wrong). The air was stale (it was cold) and suddenly (he thought he was dreaming) she took the ring off (almost angrily) and shoved it back into his hand (definitely angrily) and walked back down the trail. He stood there (unable to look back at her walking away) just stood there ("It's like trying to get rid of hiccups" his dad used to tell him during their lessons at the local recreation center) feeling defeated. He felt as if she had (she might as well have) pushed him right off the edge of the cliff. But she didn't (why wouldn't she?). It was done (they were over) and he had made up his mind (finally) and regained control of his legs again. Walking forward (he did it), he closed his eyes (au revoir) and held his breath (like his dad taught him).

rise end foul

## The High *(The Rise)*

Elevated, mind spinning like the ceiling fan. Neon colours and hues you never knew existed in the colour spectrum. You'd smoke all the colours if you could, or inject them into your blood stream. They look like they could provide a fairly decent high. The kind where you could walk on ceilings and watch yourself sitting dazed on the floor. Or walk through walls into rooms you weren't aware of before, jumping off the tallest city scrape only to find yourself at the top, only to fall again. But the colours eventually begin to fade and flake, their brilliance replaced instead with the undeniable multiplicity of black remorse. The problem with the high is always the fall.

\*

## The Low *(The End)*

Sorrow resonates from the corners of the room like a sonar, reminding you of exactly where you are. The four walls surrounding you aren't as much as your friends as you imagine them to be, it's just that you imagine them to be. The ground will tremble and the roof will collapse, bringing them down with everything else. You're very much alone, and it's time you stopped getting used to that fact and started accepting it. I promise you, you won't ever amount to anything this way.

\*

## The Medium *(The Foul)*

You're not safe here for too long. Run before you run out. All forms of comfort come with an expiry date. You should have checked for freshness before you took it off the shelf and walked over to the cashier to finalize your purchase the currency of your trust. Transaction complete. "Final sale," she said to you, but you weren't paying attention. You were too content in the moment to have processed anything at the time, confident in your choice. And now you suffer your own consequences.

## Oblivion

The stains marking my hands are stubborn,
They wish to stay rather than to wash away
The guilt marks in me a permanent place
A threshold from which it can humiliate

The little drop of water echoes in this well,
Drumming like thunder, like a lash for a blunder

The limbs and extremities that once knew life
Now know no more; for they've turned ghostly white

I'm running, still running
From what was, what is
And what always will be
And I will be, running

The truth hurts? I couldn't tell
Having been lied to so many times
You just sort of forget.
And then you realize
You forgot what you're running from

## Speaking Signs

Black leather skin woman and yellow spandex man. He sat at the table in the lounge eating his breakfast like a hungry child. She came and sat in front of him, saying, "Now, you're a handsome man!" and in response, he began waving and flailing his hands and fingers in all different styles. He tapped on his forehead and drew mystic shapes in the air, a sort of magic the leather skin woman was not exactly educated in. Though she did hear of other folk like this silent magician. She nodded at his gestures, probably thinking, "I'm sorry Mister, but I don't speak sign," but being too kind to say so out loud. So she sat there, as did he, occasionally throwing a magic spell of signs her way, and she would absorb them and return her own, more simple magic of a smile. So much was said between them at that table, without a word being spoken at all.

## Unfeeling

Do you know how it feels to feel
Like you can't feel anymore?
To go out in the winter, and
Expect the cold to bite your face
But it doesn't
To want to be kissed
By the warmth of a summer breeze
But never are

You feel alone
Like a street light on an empty road
With a red post box
Sitting right underneath
But nobody sends letters anymore
Yet you shine on with the hope
That somebody one day will
It's a good idea

This is almost what you wanted
Almost

It's ironic, you say
Silence can be loud
You are not just stuck in time
You are time itself
Standing still
Though you know you have places to go
You just need a minute

How long is a minute, anyway?

There in the winter
By the street lamp
With a red post box
Stuck in time
You dream
Or you think you do
But thinking is all that matters
Isn't it?

There you see that person
The one that comes often in dreams
The one that left you speechless
And you ask questions
The ones desperately in need of answers
The person turns away
Without a sound, this time
They are speechless

And though eyes met
Gestures, though cold, shared
In a moment in time
Transfixed
You want to forget
No, you need to
Claim back your soul
You don't want to feel

This is exactly what you wanted

## In-Convenience Store

Welcome to the inconvenience store
How may I be of disservice to you today?
What's that? Broken promises you say?
I have a fresh stock of those
and disappointment? I have a whole
shelf of those, right this way
Oh yes, of course, say no more
I have a whole section on failure, too
I've got you covered, not to worry
Lies? Got tons, get one and second is free
I've also got a whole aisle of pretenses
if you're interested
Ah! Insults! I've got a wide variety of those
Do you want mild to severe in hurtfulness?
Just let me know
I got what you need right here
And please do come back
I appreciate your business

## Time, Travail

A non-spatial cemetery, an event called for evaluation. Force spoon-fulls of time down my throat, so I can get a taste of your memories. Bitter or sweet, sour as the time when you were twelve and rebelling against the ground, climbing towering trees and breaking fragile limbs. It was around then that you discovered the sensations between your legs, a world of wonder, wandering, wondering nonetheless. We don't exist in time, we simply swim through liquid space, slithering through this thing called society, something called sense, but that which lacks that it tries to define, so therefore an absence. Or absurd. They say the more it expends the more it heals but that's a lie. The more it expends, the more a wound expands, self-inflicted but not always so, and as such there is no procedure for a reversal. Flawed in its fluidity, it waits for none while promises more but never the same. So damned to its currency, drenched in its presence. Constantly, we are moving, but really we are still.

## Hollow Cost

Lives lost, the price of life is a hollow cost. Incessant aggression, humans are insistent on becoming gods. The light is gone, the guilt on their hands will never come off. Will the violence ever stop? How much greed is considered enough? A rain of bullets and bombs are calling your bluff. The flow of their blood can never be measured in cups. Humanity has run out of luck. Fragile minds always act like they're made of tougher stuff.

*

An eye for an eye should have made us think twice. The destruction and desecration is unstoppable, yet unjustifiable. Nothing can justify the taking of one life, let alone several. Once the cycle has started, the only end is the end itself. The price of peace has inflated to the cost of violence. A most tragic, and hollow cost. A holocaust.

Definition:
capitalism

'ka-pi-tuh-li-zum' *(n):* a system of illusions that creates divide and disparity between the classes of rich and poor; a bullshit economic "system" in which the gap between the two classes grows increasingly distant; a racist system that denies both the fact that it is racist as well as the fact that its basis lies not in capital and ownership but more so on the firm grasp of classism within today's modern day society; to be born and bred under this corporate economic structure is a call for suicide.

## Pharmakon

Morphine metaphors and dopamine dreams. Cups of liquid wisdom and cans of spray paint clouds. Corrupt concepts and crystallized memories. Friend-zoned, sleepless, benzo, prozak, lithium. Fire, whiskey. Burning bridges, ablaze in passion, or animosity. Monstrosity and anonymity of secrecy. Longing, nostalgia. Unfeeling, done feeling. Comfortable, or numb. Ataraxia. Headache. Acetaminophen, again.

## Strew / Dent

They institutionalized my integrity, confined my mind and chained my dreams. They've made it hard to breathe in the city on the universe. Instruction is inefficient. I came here to learn, but all they do is teach. I need a degree to qualify my intelligence, to verify any worth. Even then, I'm not promised any brand of certainty. I am a number, an insurance policy, mere tuition fees away from living on the street, and if I achieve the latter it would be accredited to the former. These are the perils of a student.

At least give me free parking.

## Narc

I want to smoke a piece of your mind. Just a fragment. Grind it up and spark my lighter to it. Just so I can see what you see, think the way you do. Feel you within me, filling up my lungs with your lovely toxins. Over and over again. I never want to lose your high, I don't care how detrimental it may be. I'll deal with the complications, I wouldn't mind your disease. Cardiac arrest me, handcuff my heart and keep me in your hold. I'm addicted to pure bliss, sniffed from between the strands of your hair. I'm dependent on the look of your face, glimpses shot in the seconds my eyes stray from the road and dare to be locked in yours. You're a craving I need to keep fulfilled, always.

## Someone Else's Headache

I've paid my price and done my time. Faced the consequences as they were due. I can't be held responsible any more, anymore. I've shed more concern than my interest can produce, I've exhausted my emotions and overpriced my time and devotion. I can't afford to care for worthlessness, oversold and undervalued. I won't be responsible for the next stock market crash. I've cashed out my investments and sought my fortunes elsewhere, where my value exceeds my own worth. My greatest asset lies in the knowledge of character. My wealth is boundless now. And you, you're someone else's headache. Simply not mine to worry about.

## Dizzies

The tumors in your sighs give me breath cancer. And even before I could diagnose your malignance, the persistence in your eyes sends a shiver down my spine, rendering me paralyzed for life. Left speechless, you're my weakness with all that sweetness that you speak. Swiftly my soul's sifted and slipped into your gifted reach, like candy to a child (or more like sex to a freak). A fiend for your touch taste and feel, a visual meal of your sexual appeal. I'm in heat, I need more than just a peak. Label me a beast, you can destroy me but still I want your disease.

## Brand of Perfect

I take some time for reflection
as I j-walk at the intersection
Lost in retrospective introspection
You can be least respected when you least expect it
Call it sight correction, or is it just neglected
Affects of effects infected to imperfect her perfection
Got me thinking if I was a regret, or her natural selection
Because I'm adept to adapting to reject and new direction
Tainted recollection, reminiscence of all her essence
The presents of her past presence
Lingering in the back like bad math lessons
Perceived all wrong by my optic lenses,
severed peripheral view
I know my perception is influenced by affection..
But I found perfection in you.

## Distraction by
## Over Indulgence

She always keeps her socks on.

It's something I've come to admire. I didn't really notice until she pointed out the fact that feet actually do get cold. So I started to do the same. Feet are weird things, I've never really liked them. But there's a certain comfort when my feet play with hers, or just stay there still and entangled together. Other than that, they are sort of useless aside from getting me where I need to go. That's mostly to school and work, but they're more important while on the gas pedal, taking me to see her.

We lay under the covers, wrapped in the warmth of our bodies in an otherwise cold room. Ventilation problems. But our feet are always cozy, so we're happy. We talk for what seems like days sometimes, laughing, sometimes wrestling. A lot of the times just fantasizing about a strange thing called the future. We don't know what any of that means, we only have a slight idea of what it might ever entail. But the idea is sweet and we're like children crazy for candy, so it works just fine. Simultaneously, I think about how life would be if I had not met her. Again.

Scattered messages and spontaneous meetings, an all too much suppressed attraction that neither of us knew about nor tried to confirm. A brave dare, and "Challenge accepted" brought us here. New Year's fireworks went off twice; once above Main, and a second time on the corner of Queen and Theatre Lane.

My dulling flame was given life once more, licking every curve and crevice of her attention as well as her body. I empty my thoughts onto her skin, her eyes soaking in my every detail like a sponge so she can squeeze them all back out onto the paper.

Oh. She's an artist. A brilliant one, actually.

She looks up at me, with her adoring brown eyes and strawberry nose, even in heels when she stands a bit taller. My frame seems so much bigger than its limitations. I feel like a giant in her presence, and I can never deny how much I love it. My inner Leo is showing, taking center stage and demanding all her attention. After all these years, I finally love having someone's eyes continually fixed on me. It's exhilarating, the feeling described best simply as inexplicable.

We lay staring at each other, singing songs by Three Doors Down together. I sing some others, just fragments, overly cheesy. I check to see if her ears are bleeding.

Here's the thing, I know how most stories end. Now being brave enough to call myself a writer, I'm really only interested in the endings anyway. They're the only part that have ever really mattered to me. I used to be able to tell every story's ending to incredible accuracy, but I don't know how this one ends. I'm far too distracted by over indulgence to be worried about how this one ends. But maybe I don't really want it to.

Maybe it won't.

## Continent of
## Disappointment

Continent of disappointment
Disjointed visions
of foreign landscapes
Forecasting
the fall
Wax wings
will only get
you so far
until they melt
Friends are foes
well behaved
enough
to win you
over.
That's all
it amounts to
in the end.
Over.
The stubborn winds
will never
let you
leave
this place
alive.
Enjoy your permanent
home with
failure.

## ChillxIn

Can we chill, I got a couple pills, I can take you for a thrill. You know what's the deal, just tell me how you feel. Girl you're dressed to kill, I love your sex appeal and I'm just looking for a feel so you don't gotta tell me that it's real. I'll flip you and double dip you, or whatever you're into. Nothing's an issue, just don't try to make me miss you or you're gonna need some tissues.

## Coward

It was 4am as she stood in the mirror clutching her belly. Unsure of what to do, it was a bit over two weeks already. The thought of it consumed her, weighed down on her heavy. She was only seventeen and he was probably not ready. Contemplate, should she tell him or wait, or leave it up to fate? She had to make up her mind, do something before it's too late. She thought about what he would say, if it would be okay, to keep the baby that they made or let it get away. Shrinking in shame she looks for someone to blame. Because everything would change, nothing would stay the same.

It was him that said that if he loved her then why would he need a rubber. Now standing in despair she was about to become a mother. So she made up her mind that she had to let him know, before it was too late and the fetus inside her was grown. Later that day she slipped on her coat, head out the door, completely unaware of what the day might have in store.

She reached his house, rang the bell, he answered all confused. Until this day she wasn't sure how many drugs he abused. His open arms welcomed her but she just walked into the house. She stopped in the kitchen as he asked, "What's this about?" She looked away, afraid and ashamed, the words never came . She placed her hand on her stomach, then he started backing away.

"You're not serious!"

"Yes I am."

Then he said, "It wasn't me!"

She looked at him in awe, "Then who else could it be?!"

He implied she slept around and she slapped him in the face. He pushed her against the wall, dropped dishes and broke a couple plates. Said, "You better lose it, or I'll punch that thing out of you."

She said, "You wouldn't dare, even if you wanted to."

So he struck first, hard, a swift fist to her belly. She fell to the ground, the hatred in her now deadly. With hands sweaty she reached for a knife that had fallen on the floor. And when he came for the next blow she punched him in the jaw. Got up to her feet and he could see the change in her eyes. Saw the knife in her hand as she whispered, "Goodbye"

The trial convicted a seventeen year old on charges for murder. She pleaded the story in her defence but nobody heard her. Although it seems tragic, this sort of thing always happens. Victims of abuse and harassment, and *love* is the trapping. There's a lot of men who act cowardly, a lot of babies dying hourly. Hospital graves, state property of a life never lived but ended sourly.

## Diss Belief

Sharpen the image or sharpen my vision. Sharpen your claws, sharp blade incision. Sharpen your fangs and dig into my skin. Drown your beliefs, christened in sin. Drowning the bottle and making heads spin. You are a beast, and we are of kin. Mesmerized, your terror eyes tear a hole in my soul. Your hands rip open the ground and carve an image from stone. Give it the life that you breathe, but you fail to believe. You wouldn't have stayed, I knew you would leave.

## Break the Child
*For Divy*

Terror eyes only inject fickle fear, plaguing the brave. Deathly promises in a lively world, too much at stake. Too little, too soon, not enough. Break the child, traumatized in shock. Break the child, grind words until weak. Break the child, blindfold, asleep. Too young to interpret, too late to change. Break the child and mark his grave. Enslave the child, bound in chains. Apply the bleach, art is a stain. Starve the child, it's the only way. Make another child to break.

*break the child*
*crush the kid*
*let him know*
*whose world this is*

# The Rage of Achilles

.

## Kaleidoscope

You're a kaleidoscope, full of abstract shapes and colours, and things that I have never seen before in my life. You're always vibrant, full of the little things that never fail to spike my curiosity. You're full of surprises. You're a mystery to me. I'd like to know you like the back of my hand, but the problem lies in the fact that you're nowhere close to being as dull. Your smile emits colours that are likely still nonexistent on the spectrum. But by far, you're the most radiant.

## Serendipity

Am I tripping, or just drunk off your drunken kisses? You can speak, and I'll just listen, as I try to take in what I've been missing. Don't mean to flip the script but your beauty goes beyond description. I think I need a prescription to a dose of you, with your permission. Here's me subscribing to your submission, scribbling down a list of wishes. Here's to chance and its gift of giving, me the opportunity to live out a dream dreamt vivid. Not a gentleman, I'm just a kid again. Chocolate and candies flavoured with cinnamon. And trading card tournaments. Yeah, without a shadow of a doubt I think I'm living it out. I think I found the fountain of youth while I'm kissing your mouth.

## The Rage of Achilles

If the artist is born in chaos, I'll be born again in calamity. In the midst of depravity, my doubts take a stab at me. My vivid thoughts have killed off the man in me like a Greek tragedy. Call it savagery. It's not an Odyssey, it's the opposite; and Icarus isn't falling, he's burning down metropolis. So as I'm drowning in flames, I'll smile as I bleed. Scorch the velvet of dreams, as I destroy myself in the rage of Achilles.

## Faith

I used to be a nonbeliever until I found a keeper. Now I swear I'd never leave her until I meet the reaper. I'm loving all her features, she catch me staring like a creeper. But I just tell her that I need her, that I live her and I breathe her. Too much chemistry for beakers, I'm scuffing my Adidas, laces loose on my sneakers. In other words, I'm tripping; she has a way to make me weaker. In other words, she's different, all in all a keeper. She got me sweating up a fever while I dream her, so I guess I've fallen like I'm Caesar. No croutons, just kisses, and I'd rather fall and slip than try to get a grip. Because she's everything I've been missing.

## Iblis' Itinerary

Running from flames,
feet soaked in kerosene
Setting fire to
everything
with a shaking hand
and a calloused heart
Northern dreams and
southern screams
Naked palm trees
and burnt sugar canes
Smiles once used
to taste sweet

## Deepfriedlungs

Deep fried lungs in love like molasses slow poison drug gaseous killing masses similar stimulant stimulating a high elevating escalating rise respiration rate fuck an expiration date I'm immortal conversation confirmation fluidity you can ruin me you speak a kind kinda love fluently lungs in my poison too numb to feel hurt I'll race you to the sun winner burns first.

In A Better Place
*For S.H. and J.H.*

Every time I kiss her around the waist line, I think about how you would look. Would you have your mother's eyes, a little birth mark on your foot? It leaves me shook to see the kids in the neighborhood, playing with their toys and flipping through picture books. They say I can't raise a child but I think I could. I'd take a couple extra shifts at work and things would all be good. I try to blink away the tears as my heart sinks, and now and then I think about how much happiness it would bring to sing you to sleep. Suddenly you have left me incomplete, the slippery slope is steep and I'm tumbling all over the place. The child of our love, I'd give anything to see your face. With or without a name, I'll see you again in a better place.

## Sin Tax

day dreaming by the window sill having traded a few dollar bills for the cheap thrills of pretty pills shrieks and shrills this is the only time the walls actually stand still as your shrivel into the corner waiting on the coroner to come and investigate the kill the cause of the death of your mind compassion lost too young what a waste of time your brilliance became an exhausted resource frosted remorse you're a walking corpse with poison in your lungs and despair in your eyes maybe you should stop being dependent and learn to compromise

## Genius

Masterful pieces of cognitive genius scribbled between margins and creases through ink and telekinesis. Form an allegiance through appeasing to logic and reason and emotional grievance. Call it a change in the seasons, the beacon of demons is the existence of heathens. Sinners are screamers, trust me I've heard them and seen them, never to step foot into Eden because of what they refuse to believe in. I've been an elitist since a fetus, I'm the meanest genius, check my genus. My explicit simplicity reaches out to complexity seekers, exquisitely. Sadness seeps through the pores of a sleeper, fuck a crypt keeper. I'm a slick creeper blowing speakers, scuffing sneakers and setting off security beepers. Hard wood and beavers, take a plunge beneath the sheets of conscious thought until it hurts to breathe, burst a pool of genes into a moist cavity and pray she bleeds. Life and love are both a tragedy.

## Solving for $x$

The only thing that's constant is looking for a constant, in a world filled with variables. I will probably never be efficient, let alone co-efficient. I am more likely to ride these sinusoidal waves of depression until my thoughts and perceptions are reduced to a fraction. There are no reciprocals, I have no formula. No meaningful factors to stick into this equation. I'm just an anomaly, and I'm tired of solving for $x$.

## Reaching Beyond the Blue Door

*But when it's bad, it's terrible.*

The words echoed in the hall, bouncing off the walls like music, only they weren't so pleasant. It is times like these when two people become displaced as strangers, when the little spaces between them get stretched for countless miles and every room becomes a distant country.

I sit and watch as the mist swallows her and her shadowed figure begins to disappear. I try to follow for as long as I can before I encounter obstacles that I know I cannot pass. But there, I'll wait until she finds her way out again, with a hand outstretched and waiting.

Sometimes she is just within reach and I can touch her in the cloud of mist. Most of the other times, I can barely feel her against my fingertips and that's when I know she's wandered off to far, and then I worry.

I'm not sure how a single room could stretch to the size of different continents. But at times, we are on different parts of the world, different hemispheres and time zones. If I am in day, she is in night, and without her I feel equally lost.

"I'll be right here," I tell her every time. It is never a lie, because I will always wait. I will wait until the constraints of her inner conscious release her and let her come back to me. Sometimes, it takes longer than others. But I'll still wait.

"Let me be alone." The words echoed in the hall as she cast me out. I didn't want to move, refused to for the first time, though reluctant. But I did leave, stepped outside as she noisily shut the door.

I sat there like a cat scratching on her blue door, until she came back around and realized I had been waiting.

## Hurting

I look for you in every coffee shop. Thinking you'd be there in a corner somewhere, working away at your sketch book while plugged into Daft Punk. I scan faces like a thief, and I get stared back at like I really am one. But you're the thief that managed to climb over my high walls, walk through my guards, steer through my insecurities and steal the one thing I've kept protected for so long. I'm so vulnerable to you. You don't even know this fact.

## I Love Her

She's a spitting image of a goddess, modest, I'm just being honest. Chronic illness, there's a stillness in the air when she's not there but she fills it with a stare. So I thought I'd grow a pair and tell the world about this girl who fills my world, and it's rare. Because I'm a critic, often a cynic, my words are acidic but my love is painted in acrylic. You see, I'm a lover and a dreamer, because I love her and I dream her. Now I need her and I breathe her, my blood pressure off the meter. Because she's my music, my hip-hop. She's my Lauryn Hill, My BIG, Pac. A pair of fresh kicks, my wristwatch. She's my heartbeat, my tick-tock. Whether my dick hard or my dick soft. Whether we're holding hands or lip-locked. Or fussin'-fighting or criss-crossed. I mean X-and-O's, kisses on the neck and nose. Or our curled toes under covers. Even the lord knows that I love her.

## Vacancy

The road is empty now for miles, but you've left your fresh tire tracks behind. Deep marks in the cracked asphalt that are sure to stay for months to come. You checked out without a concern for the condition you left the place in. I suppose you were in a rush.

## A Week Before Wasn't This Weak

You had my walls coming down
we were the talk of the town
You wanted a noose,
but I gave you a crown
You said I was your drug
I said you were my sound
You were the one treading blue,
but I'm the one who drowned

Now I'm waking up in cold sweat
pieces of your hair on my neck
From the pillows you rested
your head on my bed
It was only a week ago
before I got this weak
Little red and the wolf
The lion and the sheep

Crying in the sheets
you fell too far beneath
You lied because you're weak
Now I know you love to bleed
and I was too in love to see
That you never gave a fuck
you just made it hard for me to breathe

## Forfeiture

Casually a casualty
I was the coffin for your causality
the comma before your coma
The crown before your noose
the guilt to your corruption
The corrosion to your steel
the bandage before the blade
I died to make you feel

## Bastard Town

I encountered desolation on my travels. The man asked me what I want here. I replied that I wasn't looking for love, but maybe a place to rest and a piping hot cup of loathing. He looked at me sympathetically, feeling sorry. You need to stop, he said. I asked him for a bottle and a cup so I could call his bluff.

## The Best Ideas

Good ideas never come to me while writing. They always come to me at any other time except for when I'm actually physically writing. The best ideas come to mind when I'm driving or while I'm stuck in deep conversation with someone. Or when I'm at work serving a customer, being watched by at least six different cameras at one time. You see, the best ideas come to mind at the very times when I am unable to write them down. So I write them in my head, repeat them over and over out loud and under my breath in a tragic attempt to memorize them. But the best ideas are always fleeting ideas. Ones that show their face once along the shore and then wash back to sea with the tide. The fragmentary ideas that remain are the sediments that I work with, write down with a sense of shame and defeat for having let the rest get away so swiftly. Once more, like every time before. That is perhaps why everything I write always feels so incomplete.

## Fatal Attraction

It's a fatal attraction, subtraction of any mental satisfaction. It's an aphrodisiac but in fact I need some prophylactics. Excuse the antics, but your tactics are distracting. So much in fact, my following actions could be real disastrous. I should have read the fine print and asterisks, but I'm like a kid out for candy so I saw it and just went after it. Need I mention that you caught my attention, and ever since that instant, there's been this intense tension. Intensified by the way you extended your glare in my direction. My intention was pure contentment, even without an erection. Your intention was inception through deception, interception of your depressive recollections. But confrontation led to us being deep in deepened conversation which was confirmation before consummation. I fell in love with a troubled mind in a troubled time. I witnessed a bit of her pain, only to double mine.

# Naked
*For E.G.*

Being naked was always scary for me. Not alone, of course, but to be naked in front of someone else meant a big deal. It meant choosing to let that someone else see me for everything I am, beneath the kind of clothes I wear. My skin has no fashion sense, it's just skin and pigmentation. But what will you make of me in my natural state? Will you understand that even before the thought of sexual pleasure is the pleasure I seek from the look in your eyes?

Being naked meant to expose my insecurities, to let you see my scars like a visitor in a museum. But I was happy to know that I wasn't the only one hiding things under my clothes. I've seen all of yours, but your scars were different. Mostly self-inflicted. I ran my finger along them, tried to imagine the pain and sting, never quite understanding, but kissed them gently anyway. You were clever about them, always bringing the blade to places that were well covered by clothes.

But I hope you know that I still loved you with all your scars. Even the new one that you lied to me about. Even the burn marks on your legs from that night in New York.

You probably don't remember that day. We were naked, and we had gotten well acquainted with each other's bodies by then. We did what two naked people do when seemingly in love with one another. I began to crumble on top of you as you held your legs wrapped around me and ushered me to my finish.

I finished, and lay there on top of you with my eyes closed, soaking in the moment. My head on your chest, ear pressed against your skin, I began tapping out the rhythm of your heart. "What are you doing?" Memorizing your heartbeat, I said. You giggled softly and asked why. I replied, so I could sample it into a song someday.

You had an irregular heartbeat. I still remember it, and I can still tap it out. You also had an irregular affection for me, and that's something I wish I could forget but I can't. Now even with clothes on, I feel completely naked.

## The Quiet

When silence is not pleasant and welcoming, it is deafening and murderous. It plants a seed of uncontrollable and irrational thoughts, growing almost instantly and constricting all sense and logic. This monstrous thought birthed from silence proceeds to feed upon your fears, growing larger still and wandering off into the depths of the abyss that you call your mind. It knows your insecurities, and as such it knows which buttons to push, which strings to pluck. It knows which images to flash before you, which voices and words to play back in your ears, and which sensations to send trickling down your spine. It knows you, and it equally knows how to torture you, ever so slowly. If you were once hungry for the silence, you are now thirsty for sound, gasping for a drop of noise in a desert of torturous tranquility. Anything to break you free from the hold of such unwanted thoughts. You'll do anything.

This is loneliness.

## Gunpowder Tea

Let's overdose until we're comatose. So morose that we never know the sight of hope. Like cocaine kisses on sunkissed skin, my lips are addicted to your addiction. Conflicted in conviction and contradiction, constricted by your corrupted system. Poor decisions, blade incisions, it's far worse than you envisioned. Your heart's a prison, distant sounds of water dripping, and I know your soul's been drowning in it ever since. If you're not convinced, it's only a matter of time until someone walks off the edge due to restricted vision.

Gunpowder tea, suicidal tendencies are surging through our entities. The blade is a false remedy, mixed melodies of a Gloomy Sunday and a masochist's hypocrisy. Don't get stuck in these, they will ruin you with no care for subtleties. Easier said than done, if you can't then just stop. If you want something that really hits the spot, go on and take a shot.

## Victim Eyes

In love with the idea of being in love. Memories as sweet as a pleasant dream, haunted by the nightmares of all the above. A tight vice grip on all senses and sensibilities, skewed perception and shattered logic. Your argument is forever invalid. The mortar shells and scattered shards of glass resemble nothing more than mortal vulnerability. Blood inches down the sleeve of the past, tossing and turning in its grave, ablaze. Its bones exposed, flesh rotting and mutilated in moral resignation. This is a cryogenic state beyond emotional hibernation. This is genocide. And you are inevitably fated to be the victim.

## Nine to Five Forever
*For Shuvo R.*

## Joe

Reluctant feet slowly stepping out of crowded dreams. Slow retreat from wisps of sleep, restlessly since the past few weeks. From Monday to Sunday, lifeless. Sunday to Monday, trying to get in the mind set. From Monday to Monday, always the same. How is it that a man walks free but is still bounded to chains? Feet swinging over, finally touching ground. Looking out the window, taking in the morning sounds. Yet still with eyes open, merely a zombie. All until that first cup of coffee.

\*

The beginning of the nine to five: waking up. Consumerist slaves driven by their savior; a black beverage extracted from roasted beans, either milk or cream, possibly sugar. And perhaps also driven by an old dream they've desperately clung on to since before they lost their compassion. Not by choice. Some still dream with their eyes open, most only with eyes closed. While some others have forgotten how to dream entirely.

## Nine to Five Forever

### Shirley

Surely she wasn't in love enough to fight for "us." Her love for lust defies his trust. But she's his crutch and for that he thinks they're in love. But she's just another office desk clerk with an amazing bust. She said their sex was nice but she liked it rough, and that he could never really please her much (she liked handcuffs and such). Stripped clothes and curled toes, sins of the un-forgiven burn slow. She's never there, but she'll never let him know. Because she needs the way he looks at her for the days she feels low.

*

The look in one's eyes has a tremendous impact. The look of admiration or jealousy, love or lust, scorn or support. The eyes are an early warning symbol of hidden intent or the indication of a genuine personality. Still, things change and circumstances are determined by multiple possible variables. All of which may not always be within our immediate control. To be easily trusting of others warrants the need to most possibly undergo a psychiatric evaluation. You're likely suicidal.

## Nine to Five Forever

### For Eva

Convicted to slaughter, mothers and fathers, sons and daughters. A personal reign of greed, wars won by machines. How much does one need? Media plants the seeds and a trigger performs the deed. Forever invested until you bleed, they're out to bring the world down to its knees. They fear the people of the masses, because the greater the support the stronger the attack is. They bait technology for attachment but to stand down could prove to be disastrous. You and I are not synonymous, in fact we're opposites. One undoubtedly negative, the other strangely positive.

*

*Forever.* That's the only certain length of the reign of terror that blindly rules over the common people. The double edged sword continually widens the gap between the rich and the poor. Although they will never be acknowledged, the impoverished serve as the pillars of capitalism, which has inevitably given birth to classism. Equality is a joke, doctrines do not protect you. The ones sworn to be your protectors don't even protect you, so how then will a piece of paper with fabricated words do anything? Forever. You don't have to live that long to feel its effects or live its consequences. If you're born in the lower end of the system, your current lifetime may have already been too long.

## Nine to Five Forever

## To: Long

Her heart's gotten tired, so she set her wrists on fire. She's one to be admired for having picked the desire. She says she's lived too long, and that life's done her wrong. She's always had it hard, it's the same old song. She's the kind of girl who never had a Barbie. She's got barbed wires around her heart and a bottle of Bacardi. Life of the party, out to take her life with a knife and a note written with a sharpie.

\*

You never have to look too hard, there's always an easy way out. The question is of whether or not it's something worth going through with, in the end.

## Nine to Five Forever

## Mary Jane on Yonge St. / Re: Pete

Leave your keys, we're going on a trip. Take another sip. If you feel it, take a hit. The lower that you are, the higher you will get. Cocaine kisses on your neck. Cum, get wrecked. You're looks are foreign, too good to be ignoring. I'm about to give you that purple label, like Ralph Lauren. Because the way you're zoning I can tell that you've been Dom Perignon-in'. I got you open, you're overdosed on serotonin, and best believe I'll have you moaning until we reach the morning.

*

Religion? No. It's selfish indulgence that is the opiate of the masses. Opt not to search for gold in the gutters. All you will ever find there is despair and the carcasses of hopes and dreams. Look within yourself for happiness, and abuse that all you may; there is no greater substance.

**

## Re: Pete

Life can prove to be mundane in all its structured routines. However, circumstances are products of variables as opposed to being predetermined, as most believe. If you wish to not repeat the banal activities life demands of you, simply do not. Take charge and initiate the cycle of change you require for yourself. And once you start, simply do not stop.

## Sick Sadness

Some people are just happier when they're sad. It's strange to actually understand, but so are people on the whole. It's a certain kind of addiction to a particular state of sadness that drives a person to go back to it, again and again, despite how detrimental it may be. Maybe it's comforting, in a twisted way, or maybe more so because that particular sadness is something that is familiar. Familiarity is important, even if it's attached to negativity, which it often is.

## Ignorant Bliss

There is really no easy answer to the question of why people do the things they do. They just do. We're always looking for an explanation of some sort, maybe because it's comforting in a way. However, knowledge can bring with it a sort of stinging pain that can't be easily forgotten. People have their reasons for doing what they do. Sometimes we don't know what that reason is, sometimes they don't either. Why not let it be? It's simpler than complicating the situation by trying to quench our curiosities. It is perhaps one of the very few times ignorance can be considered to be sheer bliss.

## Skin

Cut into my skin, into old wounds and carve out my secrets. The kinds of things I could never tell you. I can't tell you where I've been, you'll have to figure it out. They are all the kinds of things that could never roll off my tongue and escape my lips; you would have to see it for yourself. And don't worry, I know you're glaring; you don't have to say anything because there's really nothing to say. I wear my scars as a way of letting you know that I can take your inflictions. After all, you can't really hurt me. The most you can ever do is perhaps leave a mark.

## Fast Lane

Switch into the fast lane, these girls can't wait to change their last names. It's a damn shame, all depressed until the cash came. Wild things act tame, the craziest people act sane. Blow money, chase fame, #YOLO every tag name. Painted faces of hellish grace, institutionalized minds and consumerist slaves. The media has raised a generation of diabetics, and sadly everybody wants cake.

\*

The sugar coated lies of the corporate media have seduced mass populations into being hopelessly stuck in a vicious material cycle. Suddenly, everybody has been in a rush to experience things before their time. Everyone wants to experience love and relationships, sex, drugs, alcohol, partying, etc. All as soon as they possibly can, and as a result by the time they have reached their early to mid-twenties they are desensitized and their passion is gone. Because it was spent before it was due, and it becomes that much harder to really be excited about anything in the same way.

## Monste'R'Us

Self inflicted self conflictions, contradictions with no conviction. Feed my addiction, pay the dues or face eviction. Flip the script and switch the system. I said it once, you never listen. How're you going to work a puzzle with pieces missing? Christened in sin, slam the pistons. Born in mischief, horning mistress. Eyes glisten in sadness, stiff in madness not dismissed, trigger finger itching until submission.

## In Sin You Ate

I saw her in my peripheral vision, just sitting as I envisioned her stripping in the kitchen as I stiffen and grip her and kiss her on the lips and – damn. Then I turned around and my eyes touched her face and I was nearly blown away from having been blessed with such precision and grace. I had a decision to make, go up and say, "Hey, we should get coffee someday?" or "Excuse me let's go fuck and have kids and run away to a far off place?"

Decision, decisions.

## Course of Destruction

I'm trying to give it up so I can live it up. But no matter what, it seems I try to little and not enough. I could never call it selfish because I never thought it was. But I never saw it for what it is and the kinds of things it does. Falling in and out of love, dismissing some as lust. And when that won't help me feel, I just fall back onto drugs. But seeing myself through my momma's eyes, I'm no different from what I claim. I forgot from where I came and now I walk a path of shame. She told me not to let the satan in, instead I let the satan win. Forsaken from the path, now I feel the wrath of having bathed in sins. I cannot forgive me, no, I'm feeling empty. I can't find my shadow, it also probably resents me. Shit, it hurts to have to see that I've changed for the worst. Perspective is what it does, both a gift and a curse.

## Eight and Half
## Minutes Worth

It will take you more than a minute to understand, but perhaps less than that to make up your mind. About two minutes to grab the things you need, and in five minutes you'll be out the door. In your haste, you will fail to think about all that you will be leaving behind. In the wake of your rash decisions, you will encounter new forms of adversity. They will be the kinds of obstacles that will be most likely to take more than just eight and a half minutes to solve or walk away from. The consequences of actions carried out through irrational thought could quite possibly last you your entire lifetime. Be kind. Give yourself at least that eight and half minutes. Breathe.

## Beautifully Broken

I could see bits of her misery through her ripped jeans. It was all in her body language; the way her shoulder slumped and her hands fidgeted. The way her right foot would sometimes accidentally scrape the ground to her surprise as she walked, as she looked around hoping that nobody had noticed. It was in the dullness of her eyes and the emptiness of her smile. Its hollow spaces silently echoing the screams she fought so hard to keep concealed behind her teeth. I could see bits of her misery in the shy patches of her skin, conscious of the secrets they kept. I could taste the sugar coated words off her lips like a child crazed for cotton candy at the fair. But I was old enough to know better. I just never quite understood how someone so beautiful could be so broken.

## 5AM Confessional

There comes a point in the late hours of the night when the person you're texting stops replying. The most reasonable explanation would be because they fell asleep, since it is just after 5AM and not everyone's as crazy as you. It's at this time when you are suddenly overcome again by the feeling of perpetual loneliness. Not at all for the fact that there's nobody there in the moment, but more so for the fact that you're not there for yourself. You won't tell yourself that it's going to be okay because you can't. You don't know that for sure anymore. In fact, you don't know anything like you thought you did before. I'm sure you know the feeling.

Or maybe it's just me.

## Momentary Melancholy

All she wants to do is swallow my pride. She says she's got something for me between her thighs. I can see it in her eyes, no compromise, just the flames of my demise. Our bodies on fire, numb in cold desire. The need to be higher got us wired until we perspire. The coming down is when we're tired. Your lips taste like a liar, to tell them apart is a skill I've acquired but I'm sadly in love with its choir. Momentary melancholy, you told me your temple was holy. But I have reason to believe it went beyond me and me only. It's okay, I guess we all get lonely, heartbeats drumming our percussion. Steady stream of cussing when we should really be discussing. Causing up a ruckus, which means we're really fussing. With you saying things like it all meant nothing, you push all the right buttons. So tell me which nights you really loved me, on the nights we weren't fucking. Because you see everybody is in love in the moment they are cumming.

## Altruism

There are two kinds of people in the world we live in. You are either the one who gets stepped on or the one who does the stepping. If you're not one, you're automatically the other. That's the way it works. The process of advancement inevitably requires hurting select few or many. Ties are ultimately made to be severed, feelings felt to be un-felt, some things need to be sacrificed for the sake of greater individual profit. We are intrinsically beasts; it is innate within our biological nature. We can't help it. The ideal ism for so-called humanity bears no relation to religion. The ideal ism is altruism.

## Phantasmagoria:
## The Devil's Ghost

The intoxicating memories are often enough to sway one's mind and buckle the knees. Becoming drunk on the past is an acquired taste; some can hold the substance, most can't. I've left a trail of blood behind in my travels. The result of having danced with the devil's ghost are my severed toes, a constant reminder of my foolishness. But I dare not complain. Instead, I offer you to carve out my lungs to wear as a crown. I don't need them anymore; your residual air was a bit too poisonous for my liking.

## When the Clouds
## Come Crashing

We sought to make a house out of a home, a life out of love, forever out of the present. But our biggest mistake is that we never contemplate it all come crashing down. Sunny skies can still hold storms in the distance. The clouds will show no mercy.

## Eidolon

She came to me cloaked in the fragrance of an angel, her tattered wings but only added to the appeal. Her lips like lyrics, a smile sweet as a sugar coated simile, sprinkled with sparkling sequins and a taste for the strangely bizarre. Her unsuspected words planted tumors underneath the lining of my skin, assumed benign but turned malignant. She came as a cure, yet left me with a cancer. Undoubtedly, the devil gave birth to another monster.

## Flight Patterns

Caught in a fraction of attraction, our hearts under attack, this love is a contraption. I need some prophylactics, a fire extinguisher and a vendetta mask in all the action. Contracted by contact, there's little time for relaxing in the midst of flaming passion. Praying for a safe passage regardless of experience or practice. There's no simplifying the task, in her beauty I am basking. Sinful assassins, we're out to make the moment last as we spark our lighters to the gas and we're burning and crashing. We can never master it because we never read the fine print and asterisks. It's like an acid trip, we see things that aren't there and then we all turn to masochists. I claimed to have died and I was reborn like Lazarus. Fell for the trap again and it was nothing short of disastrous. These are candid confessions of lessons learned as pages burn, waging wars as the tables turn. Even through the warning and the consequence, baby I'm still just another bird.

## Peanut Butter and Cocaine
*For Kaitlin E.*

we were the perfect combination
like peanut butter and cocaine
addiction and affliction
like fire and propane
gaseous, never gracious
greatness delayed
an affection displayed
but weighed down in chains
too different in composition
that's why oil and water never mix
you're allergic to this
but I still need my fix

## Luckily, There
## Was No Blood

Hands soaked in sin, he was thirteen years old, locked himself inside the tiny storage room and all he could do was sit and stare at his hands. His hands soaked in sin. Shaking uncontrollably, weeping unknowingly. Karma would get him, he told himself. Karma would get him good. One day. Or maybe every day. For the rest of his life. It's all over. He can't undo what he did. Not with hands soaked in sin.

The policemen are gone. You can come out now.

## Hidden

There are a lot of words strung together to make a lot of sentences, pressed between a lot of pages in a lot of notebooks hidden in a lot of different places. A lot of these will never be absorbed by another pair of eyes. In fact, a lot of them won't be glanced upon again by my own. It's just a strange comfort to have them there.

## Human Idiocy

Isn't it strange? We do certain things knowing that they will inevitably hurt us, and when they do we act surprised and as if we never expected it to happen. Then we seek excuses. Then we glorify the grief, seek for comfort through contempt, reconciliation through revenge. It's a serious case of human idiocy.

## ill/ectric

I used to make your legs quiver, you used to make my spine shiver. You'd cry me a river every time we severed. I was in flight with wax feathers when you chose to get close. A hangman without a rope so you held a blade against my throat. Make me a ghost, baby, and make yourself a home. Claim the drama queen throne for own, but I hope you know you'll always wear that crown alone. I could taste a sliver of your mind every time you smiled, heart racing like the speed dial dedicated to my decimation. If I had died I wouldn't mind, I put it all behind because it would have still been better than your desecration. Your exhibitionist desperation has left me exhausted and exasperated. You're a disaster, baby, and this is my final resignation.

## thisability

torturous touch
deaf decay
your dreaded demonology
haunts me to this day
crippled by ripples
of resonating memories
in fact, your voice still
reverberates inside of me
a pen or a straitjacket
a drug or a crutch
nobody should ever
love you this much

## Voice Lust

You have the kind of voice I wouldn't mind falling asleep to. I think that says a lot, particularly because I prefer falling asleep to either silence or ambient music. But right now, I think I would prefer your resonating warmth over either of those. Or maybe I'm too sleep deprived for my thoughts to make any coherent sense at all. Yes, that must really be it.

## Figure Eights

This is obvious and goes beyond the cause for mention, I respect this blessed interception. This is inspiration consummated with proper conversation. Perhaps, in fact, it will provide for some introspection as we cut the tension and create a moment to serve for retrospection through recollection. I might admit, I've been out to inspect your words in search for some enlightenment. I've been broken hopeless in slow motion but my path still has some light in it.

## Gray Daze

You and I were out chasing ice cream trucks on bicycles as the world stuttered through its confusion. Great minds worked to solve great problems. The nature of ambivalence is one that never fades, forever plagued by clouds of smoke and rain. If only vanilla sprinkles and chocolate dip could ease the struggle. They say it isn't quite as simple.

Well, how about some ice cream anyway?

## What He Didn't Know
## Would Kill Him

He was looking real spiffy, her mind was really iffy. What if he just wanted to take a dip between her hips and split right after the quickie? But on the contrary, he grabbed her by the wrists, told her to sit, planted one on the lips and said that she's the kind of girl he'd love to marry. Said, "God gave me these broad shoulders, and you're the one I want to carry. And my heart skips, doing monkey flips, every time your name pops up on my blackberry."

So she sat there amazed, transfixed in a gaze. With so much to say but without the stomach to really say. So she reached out and touched his face wishing the truth would just fade away. She finally opened her mouth, but bit her tongue in resistance to admit. Because how could she tell the man she loves that she's pregnant with someone else's kid?

Make my night


Make me forget
make my night
to break my day
build me up
to break tear me down
do it all again
repeatedly
until I'm accustomed
to feeling numb
make my night
to break my day
so at least
I'll dream better
I just don't want
to be awake

## Echoes of Sublimity

We kept a lot of things hidden. Like the words we'd never say and the kinds of things we'd never do. All at the same time wanting to, but always knowing better. Refrain can be bittersweet because in the place of the unsaid is born silent motions and subliminal gestures. Things that say more without words than words could ever express.

The fragmentary glimpses of a world we'll be able sustain ourselves in are always riveting. The idea in itself sends a rush of adrenaline surging through our veins until our eyes glimmer with the kind of excitement children naturally exhibit. But we would occasionally remind one another to hold our composure. "Stop it," you would say, "It's embarrassing."

You were right. Being affectionate was an act of shame.

## Diamond
*For N.I.*

Converse unscripted like spitting verses in person, imperfect without revision. But I envision her words weighted with worth as I'm waiting on her to release me from this curse. I observed her curves and confirmed that her body is out of this world. If it's mind over matter, her mind is made of matter more valuable than gold, which in turn just reaffirms that she's hard to hold. If we're fated to be never, I'll just be benevolently clever and keep slipping through time's portals. Because if a diamond is forever, then hell, she must be immortal.

## Testimonial

I stay uplifted even as I'm drifting towards the southern sun, as day fades to night. I was gifted with a twisted tongue, and a knack to write. I must be colour blind because I only see things in black and white. That's either wrong or right, and moral grays. I'm searching for the light, waiting on the dark to fade. I've been through the long nights and restless days. And I've spent too much time dwelling on yesterdays. Reading through texts from my exes, reminiscence of each loss of breath. The missed steps and how hard it was to take the very next. I would say I'm blessed to have learned each and every lesson. Either distracted or distressed, but this is Life-101 and class is in session. It feels like I've been to hell and back, I've been a wreck. But I know I need it all to keep my head in check. I thought I figured myself out, I was sadly incorrect. To err is human, but it's messed up when I recollect.

## Fuck Cupid

Some people are just fundamentally stupid. I mean, if Cupid shoots an arrow, how is that cute and not just plain abusive? Somebody please hand that bitch a noose and teach him the proper way to use it. I'll personally take the measure of plucking his feathers, and then proceed to painfully force-feed him every written love letter, ever. This motherfucker thinks he's clever, making random people fall in love and shit. You make me sick, you baby-faced son of a bitch.

## To My Mother

You gave me the world,
so let me give you my word:
I'll never treat a woman
less than what she deserves.

You enabled me to breathe,
you taught me to be me.
If I could give you anything,
I would give you eternity.

Because I'm eternally grateful,
I understand I don't show it.
But at almost twenty-one years now,
it's important that you know it.

I am everything I am
because of you and only you.
You taught me the value of honesty,
so I remain to be true.

You accept my mistakes,
taught me to admit when I'm wrong.
And in my greatest moments of weakness,
you've taught me to be strong.

You gave me everything
so I wish to give you my best.
Because what you deserve is the world
and never anything less.

I could never repay you
for all the things that you've done.
But I can always try,
to be a better son.

## Not Around Here

I sincerely hope you take more pride in yourself for how big your dreams are than you take pride in how big your breasts are. I understand that some women truly believe that if they bat their eyelashes enough they can get away with whatever they want. Believe what you may, but let me tell you just once that it's not how things work around here. That's not at all how it works.

## Abusive or Therapeutic

Respect a student working for minimum wage, lost in a daze, confidence plagued and constant in rage. Counting raindrops until the pain stops, stained by the shadows of imaginary friends so he's self-proclaimed to not be sane in thought. The rage in his veins remain wild and untamed and he's bound to turn abusive unless he channels it into something a bit more therapeutic. Sometimes he grows tired but he still can't shut his eyes because his demons keep him wired and up all night. It's a fight he'd rather not fight but he's steady running towards the light.

## The Architect

Choking on the fumes
of a burning city
Hands decorated in blood
and standing in a pool
of my own
As the walls crumble
on its foundations
the flames licking
my contempt
I built this city
and she destroyed it

# New Direction

I must confess, I had my interests invested in girls with failing grades on their chests. The type to be down for occasional sex, amazing in bed, but now I'd trade it all for good conversation instead. We're on the same wave length like a pair of twins, maybe Siamese. Word to my mother I'm not packing a rubber when I say she's the only one I'm trying to please. I'm trying to get to know her from the neck up, because I've been fed up of girls in a rush to give it up. If it's too easy, I don't want it, believe me. I've been led astray by greed but I've never been needy. So I admit that I admire her for her qualities and treat her with equality. Tell her I'm headed towards the light and if she wants to she can follow me. But if I ever stray you have my deepest apologies.

## DevilxIsh

These are blatant confessions saturated in regret. I have a long list of lessons that I could never forget. And I hate to say this, but there's a couple faces I would love to give a face lift on a daily basis. Shades of black and blue and a healthy dose of contempt. But shit, I'm not god so it's not my job to make them repent. I was heaven-sent, but my actions say I'm hell-bent. I met the devil when I was 7, and him and I have been friends ever since.

# Homesick

He simply said, "Come, let's go for a walk," and I was out the door before he had a chance to put on his sandals. He instructed my brother to stay and watch cartoons or go bug mom and dad in the next room. With that we were off spiraling down the staircase of our neat little hotel.

The attendant at the front desk smiled and I nodded as we walked into the night through the glass doors. It was about 10pm and really dark out. But the air had cooled significantly as compared to the day and people were scarce along the streets so it was nice for a change.

We turned the corner and there was a little shop still open at the bottom of a building. "A packet of wasabi for the boy, a Benson for me," he said handing the man his money. He took the cigarette and reached for the lighter attached to the counter with a string. I opened the pack of wasabi-coated peas, popped a few in my mouth and instantly began to regret having done so. They weren't as strong as the kind that came in the cans that I would buy in Dhaka, but they still had a kick to them.

"You won't stop smoking?" I asked him for about the umpteenth time on my visit as we began crossing the street.

"You shouldn't start."

My mom's brother was two years older than her, but to me he was the closest thing to a best friend. He would take me around the city, show me the places my parents would meet secretly while they were "dating," he would even show the houses of his old ex-girlfriends. And some explicit details of the latter which he told me to never mention to anyone. It was fair and all in the past because he finally settled down and had two kids. I think he added some parts to keep me from getting bored at times.

"What are we doing here at the beach at night?" I inquired.

"*Are!* Stop asking. Just see," he said. "You spent all day in the water, now experience it at night."

One major relief was finally being able to walk in the sand. My brother and I had spent all day prancing up and down because of how hot the sand was from the scorching Bangladesh sun. We suddenly stopped walking and just stood there a couple feet from the water.

"See?" he said.

"Na, I don't see anything!"

He told me to be quiet and my eyes slowly started to adjust to the darkness around us. To my amazement, there were dozens of people still on the beach, walking and sitting, talking and singing songs.

"This is actually amazing," I said. "This is actually better than in the day!"

I could just barely make out his smile under the light of the moon. "Look," he pointed out into the water. There were people in the water, too, several feet away from where we were standing.

I visited Cox's Bazar once before with my parents in 1993, when I was about two years old. That was seventeen years ago and the only reminders of that trip were in photographs. But to experience the place in person and at an age to be able to remember it later was completely different.

I began to wonder if people always sounded so happy there. "I want to live here." I told him. "It's *perfect*."

"Maybe one day," he said. "Get a good job and buy a house here in Chittagong."

Or in Dhaka.

## TripxIn

I'm so amazed by the way her eyes glaze bright like the sun's rays. I'm giving chase thinking about how her lips taste, so ablaze with passion. My mind says to relax but the beating of my chest is a call to action. I know for a fact that a fraction of a attraction can be fatal, and lead to a need for labels. But I'm known for taking risks. This could be disastrous and I don't mean to trip, but she's like a slice of heaven with an asterisk and I'm steady going after it and praying I don't slip.

## In Other News

Congratulations, we're raising a generation of babies in hate, saturated in mindless infatuation. Isn't it great, the value of human life has been desecrated and replaced by the material things that people foolishly chase. Living on borrowed time with a lack of valid conversation as hollow minds are consumed in either thoughts of getting wasted or partaking in penetration. Occupied in vacant occupations, we live in a generation gone to waste where to no one's amazement, staying stupid is the new sensational craze.

So what good is potential without possibility?

## Cold Comfort

We are victims of convenience
crippled by circumstance
Plagued with the failure to comprehend
Or perhaps simply refusing to understand
As we are crushed in the cataclysm
and cursed to roam the catacombs
of cold forlorn memories
Words of comfort used to come easy
but nowadays they are
more accustomed to getting caught
in our throats

# ABOUT

Naveed Abdullah Khan was born in Dhaka, Bangladesh in 1991. His parents migrated to Canada in 1995. He currently lives in Toronto. He is a university student working towards a degree in English Literature.

6422717R00144

Made in the USA
San Bernardino, CA
10 December 2013